Archaeological Theory in a Nutshell

To the memory of

Dave Fredrickson
Vera-Mae Fredrickson
Jim Deetz

Their influence on my life and work was immeasurable.

Without them I'd probably be a lawyer.

Archaeological Theory in a Nutshell

WRITTEN AND ILLUSTRATED BY
ADRIAN PRAETZELLIS

Left Coast Press Inc.

Walnut Creek, California

LEFT COAST PRESS, INC.
1630 North Main Street, #400
Walnut Creek, CA 94596
http://www.LCoastPress.com

ISBN 978-1-62958-158-3 hardcover
ISBN 978-1-62958-159-0 paperback
ISBN 978-1-62958-161-3 consumer eBook

Library of Congress Cataloging-in-Publication Data on file.

Printed in the United States of America.

♾™ The paper used in this publication meets the minimum requirements
of American National Standard for Information Sciences—Permanence of
Paper for Printed Library Materials, ANSI/NISO Z39.48–1992.

CONTENTS

ACKNOWLEDGMENTS

I got a theory: it might be bunnies.

Joss Whedon, *Buffy the Vampire Slayer*

I had worked on this book intermittently for some time before getting the opportunity to complete it as part of a sabbatical leave generously awarded by Sonoma State University. To finish up, I took several brief escapes from the demands of my work at SSU's Anthropological Studies Center (which didn't stop for a mere sabbatical) to 'undisclosed locations' disconnected from phone, email, and the rest. Many thanks to Loysie and John, Maria and Tony, and Doug and Sharon for lending me their getaway places.

Of course, none of this would have been possible without the support and patience of Mary, my friend, colleague, and loving companion for more than 40 years. Thank you!

Adrian Praetzellis
Cloverdale, California
November 10, 2014

CHAPTER 1
HOW THEORY WORKS

He who translates entirely literally is a liar,
while he who adds anything is a blasphemer.

Tosafos Megillah

What this book's about

Theory is the eat-your-vegetables part of archaeology. Everyone says it's good for you, but actually getting it down isn't considered much fun.

Before the arrival of books like Matthew Johnson's excellent *Archaeological Theory* (as well as my own more modest *Death by Theory*), university courses in theory generally assigned mostly classic articles. And that is good. Everyone should read Lewis Binford's *Archeology as Anthropology* and Ian Hodder on symbols. But however virtuous it is to read the stuff, actually grinding through their sometimes convoluted (Binford) and abstract (Hodder) language has sent generations of graduate students running for the door. The same goes for those edited

Archaeological Theory in a Nutshell: Adrian Praetzellis, 9–28.

volumes of essays by recognized experts in various fields that are supposed to provide students with an overview of theoretical topics. These people know their stuff inside out—and that's the problem. Their understanding is so deep it's intuitive. Their explanations are packed with allusions that pass over the head of the beginner.

And then there's the issue of **TLDR**.[1] This internet acronym for *too long, didn't read* implies either that a post is excessively wordy or that the reader just doesn't have the time or interest to plow through it. Either way, it didn't get read, and this is surely the fate of a lot of theory articles assigned to students.

When we combine overly complex readings and short attention spans we end up concealing how archaeologists know what they know and mystifying archaeology's logic rather than opening it up. What is mystification? It's how those in authority keep the rest of us in a sense of awe about what they do, making it seem overly complex and hard to understand. It's the attitude of 'don't you worry your pretty little head about this—you couldn't possibly understand.' But archaeology is not rocket science (for which I'm very grateful). If I can understand how it works, so can you. If academic prose were the most effective means of communication, art and poetry would be redundant, which they're not.

How do I propose to demystify archaeology? Well, not by suggesting that archaeology is easy, but by emphasizing that it is carried out by people who bring multiple aspects of themselves to the practice.

Why do I propose to do it? Because one of archaeology's most important goals is (in my opinion) to reveal the processes of ordinary lives, to democratize the past. I hope to do something similar with theory itself in this book by presenting the topic mostly in plain language and by using readily understandable examples.

---

1 By the way, words and phrases in **bold** face are explained in Chapter 15.

Why archaeology is practiced how it is

In a practical sense, people do archaeology by applying

◎ approaches or techniques (such as faunal economics)

to

◎ themes or issues (like deconstructing the idea of the urban slum)

by means of

◎ theories or ideas about how the world works (such as those of **Foucault**).

It would be nice and intuitive if we could put these things in a hierarchy (like I just did) and say that archaeologists begin with a theme they want to study, investigate it using a technique, and interpret the outcome by applying a theory. And that sometimes really happens.

More often, actual studies tend to emphasize one or two of the above and give little attention to the others. This isn't a criticism, just an observation. Perhaps it's good that while we recognize the structure, we are allowed the autonomy to decide where we'll put our effort. Among some, research design has a bad name because of the practice of **front-end loading**, whereby the beginnings of some archaeological articles are heavily larded with references to up-to-the-minute social theory that prove to be worthless in understanding the discoveries made at the site.

Archaeology involves two processes (actually it involves a lot more but I'm making a point here):

◎ collecting the information—through survey, digging, and in the lab

◎ interpreting the information—deciding what it means so that we can present our story to an admiring world.

Fairly straightforward, yes?

Intuitively, it would seem to make sense that archaeologists would work by accumulating more and more facts about a subject until they know pretty much everything that can be known. For example, if you want to find out how a town grew up from a couple of houses at a crossroads, you might systematically excavate it until it's all exposed. This is what philosopher of science Thomas Kuhn calls "knowledge building." You learn more and more about a subject, adding incrementally to the knowledge base, until TA-DA! you understand it. It's basically a linear process whereby you apply a technique to a problem and interpret the outcome by means of a theory. This **normal science** model eventually results in a solution and everyone goes away happy.

That's how it's meant to happen, but the real world is a lot messier. Rather like this:

The history of archaeological thought in a nutshell

Many archaeologists are trained as anthropologists and like to see the pattern in human behavior. They also like the concept of evolution—how new patterns develop out of existing ones. If you put these two together it's clear why most histories of archaeology tell the story something like this:

◉ In the beginning, people were interested in historical explanations and so emphasized what happened when, where, and to what group in the past. They called it **culture history**.

◉ Next came the New Archeologists who wanted to understand the cultural processes involved in *why* things happened. And it was called **processualism**.

◉ Now (says the book) we're in a **postprocessual** era in which archaeologists go after a range of topics and approaches.

Like all generalizations, this one skips over a lot of detail in order to create a coherent story. That's what generalizations are for. However, the master narrative I've summarized gives the false impression that these transformations in archaeology had purely intellectual roots—that someone wrote an article that changed everyone's minds and all of sudden things were different. This view of how archaeology changed and why modern archaeology looks the way it does sounds like it should be correct. But it is deceptive in its simplicity.

The theory bit is only part of the story. But for better or worse, it's the subject of this little book, and since you bought it, we should get on with it.

Culture history...

... is where archaeology began and is still probably what most archaeologists do most of the time. Imagine the world a couple of hundred years ago: before the time of memory and written accounts human history was pretty much a blank page. Yes, there are lots of what we call archaeological sites and artifacts, but without a method of figuring out what they mean, the past (and particularly the distant past) was unapproachable. Prehistoric North Americans, for example, had created few written sources. And yet there was a huge variety of artifacts and indigenous cultures for which archaeologists had to account.

So, starting from scratch these early archaeologists had to figure out the most fundamental facts of human history: what happened, to whom, when, and where. These are the basic questions of the culture history approach, and you can't do any kind of archaeology without this knowledge base.

From the biologists, archaeologists learned that you have to classify things to understand their relationships to each other. Christian Thomsen's famous division of Danish artifacts into stone, iron, and bronze was one of the first attempts to order artifacts by material to some other characteristic—in this case, time—and the result was the now familiar names of past human eras: the Stone, Iron, and Bronze ages. This idea that collections of objects represent definable groups of people at particular times and places in the past is a **normative** view of culture and is the basis of the culture history method.

The archaeologists of the early and mid twentieth century developed methods such as typology, seriation, and controlled excavation. They became experts in classifying objects, creating elaborate hierarchies of classes, types, and subtypes, and comparing them across space and time. Familiar concepts like archaeological **horizon** and **tradition** were developed. Projectile points and pottery styles were popular as they were seen to change over time and by location. Assemblages of distinctive artifacts that co-occurred in different archaeological sites were organized into archaeological cultures. These assemblages were organized to show the relationships of archaeological cultures across time and space.

Of course, the people who were actually doing this work didn't think of themselves as doing 'culture history.' That label was invented later. If you had asked, they would have said they were just doing archaeology.

By the mid twentieth century, archaeologists had reconstructed basic chronologies in many parts of the world. And you'll recall that because they were starting from scratch, these archaeologists were mostly interested in basic information about the past: what happened, to whom, when, and where.

Although the 'why' part of the equation was a secondary concern, they hit upon the idea of diffusion to explain change. This accounted for the spread of ideas from one group to another but didn't explain what stimulated innovation in the first place. Walter Taylor's 1948 monograph, *A Study of Archaeology*, got people thinking that archaeology would never work out what causes cultural groups (in general and across time) to change without a new approach. And that had to begin by questioning some of the old assumptions.

Among these was the idea that the 'cultures' devised by archaeologists in the early and mid twentieth century were actual historical groups of people. The normative approach encouraged archaeologists to think of their constructions as having a reality. Concepts like 'the Beaker Folk' or 'the upper Archaic' had become reified, and the idea that these were merely archaeologists' abstract creations would have undermined the entire structure. The discussion came to a head in the mid-1950s in a back-and-forth series of articles between Albert Spaulding and James Ford. In short, Spaulding claimed that archaeologists' types represented the cultural categories of their makers, while Ford argued that they were useful inventions. There was more to it than that, of course, but you get the idea, I hope.

The outcome was a growing sense of unease on the part of many archaeologists (particularly Americanists) that their traditional approach had intellectual problems. What many had assumed to be a rational workman-like way of going about their work was turning out to have been rather naïve. Archaeology's 'age of innocence' was coming to an end.

Induction, deduction, and the scientific method

These early archaeologists' method was basically **inductive**. That is, they accumulated information, organized it, and came up with a plausible explanation for the patterns they observed. New information either fit into an existing scheme or was used to develop a new one. The correctness of one's conclusions was judged by consensus: whether or not other archaeologists took them seriously and used them in their own work. The approach was commonsensical and, like many things we take for granted, was peppered with questionable assumptions about the relationship between data and conclusions.

The problems pointed out by people like Taylor and Ford encouraged some archaeologists to begin to adopt the hypo-thetico-deductive method of the natural sciences—often called just the **scientific method**. While induction begins with a pile of information and ends with an idea, **deduction** does exactly the reverse.

Deduction
  ◉ starts with an idea about some characteristic of the world (a theory)
  ◉ devises a corollary that can be field tested (an hypothesis)

The field data either
  ◉ confirm the hypothesis or don't confirm it

If the data confirm the hypothesis
  ◉ the theory is supported (but not confirmed)

If the data don't confirm the hypothesis
  ◉ the theory isn't supported and may in fact be refuted

This is a huge difference from inductive thinking. The scientific method requires that I am explicit about what I want to know, how I will go about my work, and—most importantly—*how I know if I'm right or wrong*. The scientific method also requires me to lay out every detail to show how I got to my conclusions, which gives others a way to judge the quality of my work. It doesn't allow me a logical 'black box' where I can manipulate data so that they pair nicely with my conclusions.

The hypothetico-deductive (scientific) method is often linked to the next important approach in archaeology... processual archaeology.

Processual archaeology

I've said how some archaeologists began to be dissatisfied. While their anthropologist colleagues were busy identifying the common features of human culture worldwide, the traditional culture history approach still explained the past as a series of unique events—wars, migrations, new technologies, and so forth—and fixated on chronology and artifact typologies. But some new archaeologists (the movement is called the **New Archeology** in North America) took up the call by Walter Taylor and later by David Clarke in the UK to figure out *why* cultures changed. Not some particular group, but human culture in general. Archaeology, they thought, should not be the study of isolated societies but of the general cultural processes that govern all groups through time.

These new thinkers weren't satisfied to define a culture as nothing more than a particular assemblage of objects. Instead, they saw artifacts as reflections of total cultural systems. Taking their cue from the biologists, these archaeologists began to see human cultures as natural adaptive systems in which politics, economics, symbolic systems, and all the rest are bound up in a reciprocal relationship. The better the elements of the system worked together, the more adaptive (successful) was the society.

This interest in culture as *process* gave the movement its name: processual archaeology.

The idea of a human **cultural ecology** (see Chapter 2) was based on the necessity to adapt to various environments across time and geography. It would become the basic theory that could be investigated by hypotheses that related to particular archaeological cases. Through the New Archeology's concern with the general causes of cultural change, deduction came to be its basic method.

New Archeology theorists like Lewis Binford influenced how archaeologists thought about their goals. At the same time, Michael Schiffer (another American) was looking at the nature of archaeological sites themselves, not just the characteristics of the artifacts. He emphasized that archaeological sites don't just happen. They are the result of certain predictable natural and behavioral processes. Schiffer's idea was that we must understand how the dirt and the artifacts got there in order to understand a site and to know what the artifacts mean. The new generation of archaeologists controlled the quality of their data (an important aspect of the scientific method) using Schiffer's ideas.

The New Archeology's emphasis on theory transformed how a lot of archaeology was done in the 1960s and 1970s. Its influence was greatest in North America, and culture history continued to be (and still is) important in Europe and parts of the world where cultural chronology was still being refined. Many archaeologists incorporated the parts they felt were useful, ignored the rest, and went on about their own research interests. Archaeologists in Eastern Europe and Russia, whose work was controlled by the ideologies of the soviet state, knew little or nothing of the new movement. But some people who paid attention to these things were getting restless. They were increasingly influenced by an intellectual movement that had emerged from post-war France... postmodernism.

Postmodernism, postprocessual archaeology, and hermeneutics

The essence of modernism is that we can discover the guiding principles of reality by intellectual and scientific study, that we can know things with certainty, and that facts exist separately from our perceptions of them. It was claimed that in the same way users of the scientific method can understand how nature works, we can also figure out why human history and culture is the way it is.

Postmodern thinkers questioned all that. Particularly the assumption that it's valid to apply a method designed for the natural sciences (chemistry, physics...) to human society, which is eminently messier, since populations don't always do what's best for them. In fact, postmodernists questioned whether the explanations of the past provided by the scientific method explained anything at all. The past, they said, isn't over and done with. It's a moving target that is constructed differently depending on the point of view of the investigator. And most revolutionary of all was the idea that artifacts are like written texts, in that they are also open to a variety of readings (see Chapter 10). Taken to extremes, responded the modernists, this is a hyper-relativistic position in which there is no 'truth,' merely an endless number of perspectives. (This has never seemed to me to be a satisfactory critique as no one actually lives as if that were reality. Life requires that one make decisions.)

As postmodern ideas got a foothold in archaeology they began to lead the field away from the supposed scientific certainty of processual explanations. They didn't need much help. North American historical archaeologists had been so taken with the rich contexts of their sites and the potential use of archaeology in the politics of American cultural diversity (see Chapter 4) that few embraced processualism in the first place. But it took a British archaeologist, Ian Hodder, to make the break explicit in the 1980s. Rather than claiming to definitively *explain* the origins of institutions and the meanings of things, the postprocessualists offered interpretations from a variety of perspectives—including those described in later chapters.

Instead of a model based on the method of the natural sciences with their more or less unambiguous data, the postprocessual approach emphasized a continuous back-and-forth between ideas and new information. Ideas were not 'tested,' and there was no final conclusive 'answer' to most research questions. Rather, we are offered a series of increasingly sophisticated interpretations. This approach, called **hermeneutics**, is based on the idea that many complex questions can never be finally resolved by a definitive 'answer' but must be continually reassessed in the light of new understandings. That process is called the 'hermeneutic circle.'

One effect of all this was on the scale of archaeologists' research questions. The processual approach had encouraged a general feeling that every archaeologist could (and should!) take on big questions of environment, adaptation, and culture process. Postprocessual archaeologists backed off from that position, preferring to interpret particular contexts (sites) from whichever particular theoretical approach seemed to offer the biggest return (see Chapter 15). Some saw this as a step backward from the scientific approach of processual archaeology, which saw archaeology as contributing to an accumulated knowledge base on important topics. Others claimed that the postprocessual method merely recognized uncertainties overlooked by the processualists.

And now a sum up

Here's a summary of the three approaches I've just described.

	Culture History	Processual	Postprocessual
Goal	Description	Explanation	Interpretation
Method	Induction	Deduction	Hermeneutic
Epistemology (theory of knowledge)	Commonsensical	Modernist	Postmodernist

If it makes sense, you're a good abstract thinker. However, to most readers these ideas are hard to grasp without concrete examples. But fear not. That's why I wrote the rest of this book!

In the world of real archaeology (in contrast to the generalizations of textbook writers) people are still very much interested in pursuing some of the same big issues identified by processualists, such as why complex societies develop. In fact, my example in Chapter 2 deals with that very issue. And whether or not it's an example of processual archaeology doesn't really seem to matter. Archaeologists don't take on theoretical approaches like you'd sign up for a class or gym membership. People often incorporate an approach or apply a theory without referencing where they came up with the idea. When we say that Smith is a something-ist, she may object to being typecast. There's no such thing as the Theory Police to make sure everyone fits into the box. That said, academicians usually signal where their sympathies lie by whom they cite in their opening paragraphs. This is the equivalent of putting on a uniform—it positions their work within the **discourse**.

Interpretive theories and models

Take a few moments to look at this painting, "The Ambassadors," by Hans Holbein (1533).

Now hold the book up and look across it at eye level. See the skull?

The skull was there when you looked at the picture the first time, but you could only see it by changing your angle of view. Clever, eh? And this visual metaphor speaks to archaeological interpretation from the postprocessual perspective, for there are endless ways of looking at objects and situations. In fact, if I were being really pedantic I'd say that everyone has his or her own perspective. Everyone, as they say, is entitled to his or her own opinion, but that kind of ultra-relativism just puts an end to the conversation and is not at all useful. We can't just throw up our hands and say we'll never know.

This leaves us with an important insight brought to us by the postprocessualists:

> Although there are infinite individual perspectives and many different ways of understanding, clever people have found that *some ways are more helpful than others* in our quest to understand why people do what they do and why human history looks the way it does.

I outline some of these useful ideas in this book. We call them theories. If that word is still too intimidating, you can call them perspectives. Each is an idea about how the world works but, taking the hermeneutic approach, none is a complete depiction of that reality. Famous Spanish artist Pablo Picasso wasn't thinking of archaeological theory when he said, "Art is the lie that tells the truth." His expressionism wasn't interested in reproducing realistic copies of reality on canvas. He wanted to get at the essences of things.

Interpretations are lenses through which we see different aspects of the same situation. So different data sets observed through a single perspective will come up with similar interpretations. We can often anticipate an archaeologist's interpretation based on his or her theoretical lens. In postprocessual archaeologies the 'answers' to research questions are to some degree predictable. This makes these archaeologists' answers less important than how they got there and the strength of the connection they made between their data and their idea.

"It was in the latter part of the August of 1844 that I accompanied Lord Albert Conyngham…for the purpose of opening a large Roman barrow.…We were visited with a heavy shower from the south-west, when the only shelter near was afforded by the hole we had ourselves dug in the mound in which we managed so to interlace parasols and umbrellas…"

(Thomas Wright, "The Wanderings of an Antiquary" from *The Gentleman's Magazine and Historical Review, 38*, December 1852.)

Statements from the more scientifically inclined archaeologists have none of the awkward parenthetical qualifiers of some of the postprocessualists. The unity of their vision is more appealing than the fragments of perception offered by the other side. They speak with a confidence that generates trust. Conversely, reading the postprocessualists' work sometimes leaves you scratching your head and asking "What did *that* mean?" I've learned to approach this writing with the expectation that not all of it will make rational sense. Gordon Tucker wrote that some prose is "intended not so much as a cognitive experience as an empathic one." He wasn't thinking about archaeology but the idea is helpful all the same. Sometimes a writer will just get carried away. There's meaning in what he or she has written, but the significance of the words can be in their cumulative effect or their juxtaposition. If we could express all our ideas in narrative, there'd be no need for poetry—which there is.

If normal science or some approximation of it appeals to you, some of the ideas in this book will seem like tautologies, intellectual dead ends that merely confirm what we already thought we knew. I don't ask you to agree with any of these ideas or how the archaeologists have applied them. To understand what they have to say it is better to adopt an attitude of **indeterminacy**—the intellectual equivalent of the anthropologist's **cultural relativity**.

With all the approaches I describe in this book, it's no more virtuous to promote one than any other—although you'll find some are more useful. Considering the vast range of human experience, wouldn't it be strange if we all fell in lock step behind a single idea or all spoke the same intellectual language?

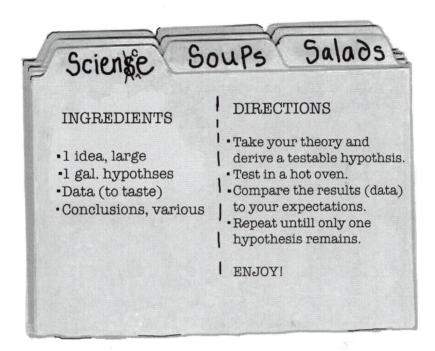

Science · Soups · Salads

INGREDIENTS

- 1 idea, large
- 1 gal. hypothses
- Data (to taste)
- Conclusions, various

DIRECTIONS

- Take your theory and derive a testable hypothsis.
- Test in a hot oven.
- Compare the results (data) to your expectations.
- Repeat untill only one hypothesis remains.

ENJOY!

How to make Science. The scientific method involves testing ideas in a way that they can be confirmed or denied. To what degree is archaeology (or parts of it) a scientific pursuit? We certainly use techniques borrowed from the sciences, but the goals of many archaeologists are quite humanistic.

Questions to Discuss

Why do some archaeologists find theory very important and others don't? What are the advantages and disadvantages of approaching research from a specific theoretical model versus without any?

Why can't we just apply common sense to what we dig up and get rid of the theory stuff?

How does explanatory/interpretive theory differ from the ideas we use to practice archaeology (middle range theory, stratigraphic theory, etc.)?

What is the role of archaeological theory in relation to archaeological practice?

Archaeologists have borrowed most of their theories from sociology, history, politics, and so forth. Is there anything wrong with that? Is it actually a good thing?

Why are modern archaeologists so obsessed with theory when for the field's first century practitioners seemed content just to do archaeology rather than talking it to death?

To what degree is archaeology a science? What makes some kinds of archaeology more like science than others?

Is knowledge building a good way to do archaeology? The only way? What other options are there?

How has archaeological theory changed over time? Do new ideas ever truly supplant existing ones?

If archaeologists' theories are just perspectives on the past and there is no objective 'truth,' why aren't the ideas of the person on the street just as worthy of study as those of some professor with Ph.D. after her name? How do we decide whose ideas are legitimate and whose are just flaky? (Did aliens build the pyramids?)

Things to Read

Binford, Lewis

1962 Archaeology as Anthropology. *American Antiquity* 28:217–225.

Clarke, David

1973. Archaeology: The loss of innocence. *Antiquity* 47:6–18.

Flannery, Kent

1982 The Golden Marshalltown. *American Anthropologist* 84(2):265–278.

Ford, James

1954 Spaulding's Review of Ford. *American Anthropologist* 56(1):109–112.

Glassie, Henry

1975 *Folk Housing in Middle Virginia.* University of Tennessee Press, Knoxville.

Hodder, Ian

1982. *Symbols in Action.* Cambridge University Press, Cambridge, UK.

1991 Interpretative archaeology and its role. *American Antiquity* 56(1):7–18.

Johnson, Matthew

2010 *Archaeological Theory: An Introduction.* Blackwell, Oxford, UK.

Kuhn, Thomas

1972 *The Structure of Scientific Revolutions.* University of Chicago Press, Chicago.

Praetzellis, Adrian

2003 *Dug to Death: A Tale of Archaeological Method and Mayhem.* AltaMira Press, Lanham, Massachusetts.

2011 *Death by Theory: A Tale of Mystery and Archaeological Theory*. AltaMira Press, Lanham, Massachusetts.

Schiffer, Michael B.
1972 Archaeological Context and Systemic Context. *American Antiquity* 37(2):156–165.

Taylor, Walter
1948 *A Study of Archaeology*. Memoir 69. American Anthropological Association, Menasha, Wisconsin.

Trigger, Bruce
2006 *A History of Archaeological Thought*. Cambridge University Press, Cambridge, UK.

Watson, Patty Jo, Steven A. Leblanc, Charles L. Redman
1971 *Explanation in Archeology; An Explicitly Scientific Approach*. Columbia University Press, New York.

CHAPTER 2

NEOEVOLUTIONISM

[Culture is] man's extrasomatic means of adaptation.

Leslie White

What is neoevolutionism?

Neoevolutionism is a bunch of ideas, based on Darwin's theory of evolution by means of natural selection, that try to explain how societies change from simpler to more complex structures. The 'neo-' part comes out of the desire to separate the modern practice from that of the nineteenth century, which arrived with a mound of undesirable baggage. You see, although Darwin proposed evolution as a biological mechanism, theorists soon extended it into the realm of society and culture with mixed outcomes.

Consider this: as the theory of evolution is such a powerful way of explaining the diversity of the natural world (birds, beasts, plants), why shouldn't it also explain the variation in human cultures? Initial attempts were not happy.

Archaeological Theory in a Nutshell: Adrian Praetzellis, 29–40.

As soon as people started to travel to faraway places and meet folk who were unlike themselves whom they classed as **Other**, they began to place them on a scale with themselves at the top. In the mid nineteenth century, Lewis Henry Morgan classified societies as being in a state of either savagery, barbarism, or civilization according to the sophistication of their technology. Every society, he claimed, passed through (evolved, one might say) these stages in order. You won't be surprised to learn that Northern Europe and white America were considered the apex of civilized nations.

At the same time, Englishman Herbert Spencer added the idea of progress from simpler (lower) forms of society to more complex (higher) forms. According to Spencer, natural selection would inevitably lead to the domination of societies and individuals who are more 'fit' in evolutionary terms. This idea came to be known as "social Darwinism" and essentially gives those at the top of the social ladder the natural right to be there. Friedrich Nietzsche's idea of a "superman" was one outcome of this way of thinking, which can also be found in the writing of Jack London. Morgan's unilinear evolution model had been abandoned by the early twentieth century but Spencer's ghost haunts the halls of power to this day.

Tainted for a while with the self-serving racism of the previous century (a legacy anthropologists still struggle against), the potential of Darwin's model to help us understand culture as a non-biological form of adaptation was just too strong to abandon altogether. If you think of humans as just another group of beasts out in the jungle trying to survive as a species, the individual cultural traits of any society (their particular ways of doing things) can be seen as adaptive responses to their own natural environment. This **cultural ecology** assumes that societies act rationally, developing cultural practices that will encourage the most efficient use of their natural environment in the long run. It's a powerful idea and worked really well in Julian Steward's studies of hunter-gatherers in the American western desert.

But good ideas don't just catch on because, well, they *are* good ideas. It's worth noting that cultural ecology arrived in the post-WWII era. At this time, at least part of the world was ready to throw out the idea that humanity is a special case among creation—that humans are in charge of their own history and may do whatever they want with impunity, such as hunt species to extinction, pollute the oceans, and explode nuclear weapons. Rachel Carson's 1962 book, *Silent Spring*, for example, shocked America with its exposé of the environmental effects of pesticides. The idea of ecology insists that humankind is part of an interconnected system of natural and cultural forces that can fall out of balance with terrible results.

But, sez you, if cultures are so well adapted to their environments, why would they change? I mean, most of the world's people are not hunter-gatherers—their societies *have* changed. Good point. Leslie White came up with the idea that societies become more and more complex as they are able to harness more and more energy by improving their technology eventually becoming... us.

These early theorists saw adaptation as directional. It had a goal in mind. Modern neoevolutionists see adaptation as more opportunistic. Adaptive success is a measure of how well a society copes with its problems at a particular point in time. Some dispense with the idea of cultural evolution altogether, claiming that it's a misuse of Darwin's term.

Neoevolutionism and archaeology

Archaeologists made a lot of use of the cultural ecology idea. And since the idea as conceived by Julian Stewart apparently has clear material correlates (actual artifacts you can find in the dirt, count, and compare), it caught on. The New Archeologists in their quest for a science of archaeology saw the approach as a way to develop 'hard' data about big important issues. And pleased with this shiny new theory, they went along quite happily.

Well, no. That's not quite right. Cultural ecology's **teleology** was clear from the start. Teleological claims in archaeology are easy to spot: when a culture is said to do things in 'in order to' or 'with the purpose of' achieving some goal, like reproductive success of which its members are unaware, you know you've got a problem. Teleological models are very seductive because they tie up the loose ends with a single grand idea or **meta-narrative**. The reason they seem to work is because intention is deduced from outcome. The logical loop is closed. Simplistically applied, models like these have a kind of inevitability about them. Societies naturally 'evolve' in a particular direction—towards complexity—without regard to inconvenient historical events or human **agency**.

But, sez you, Darwin didn't say that increasing complexity (the biological analog would be speciation) is the one and only trajectory. True, true. And therein lies a lesson for modern society out of what some archaeologists call the Classic Maya Collapse. Colin Renfrew pointed out that the Maya people had a pretty stable relationship between their population size and the natural resources available to support it. Over about 2,000 years they developed a very complex social structure, a bureaucracy, massive architecture, sophisticated arts, and so forth, and everything was fine. Well, not really. According to Renfrew, the problem started and ended when Maya agriculture couldn't support the Maya population any longer. Farming methods had degraded the environment, and over about 200 years Maya civilization fell apart—and that was that.

Or not.

Maya people didn't just fade away. They stayed around and simply changed the scale of their societies and their agriculture. Their societies adapted to the new conditions by getting *simpler*. Neoevolutionary theory assumes that societies adapt and take on new structures—sometimes more complex, sometimes not. But unlike earlier evolutionary models it isn't **deterministic**. It allows for historical accident and the influence of individuals, and may account for some of the big changes in what we call human history.

Ann Axtell Morris draws Maya glyphs at *Chichén Itzá*, ca. 1924. Sylvanus Morley (known as "Vay") directed excavations at this Maya site famous for its sophisticated architecture, art, and *stelae* (carved columns).

An example of neoevolutionary archaeology[1]

Pat Kirch has a lot of nerve. And I mean that in a good way. For many years scholars have written about pre-contact societies of Hawai'i as chiefdoms. Then along comes Kirch who says they were kingdoms. Big deal, replies 99 percent of the population. What's the difference and why does it matter anyway?

---

1 Patrick Kirch, *How Chiefs Became Kings* (2010).

'Chiefdom' is a way of describing societies that are larger and more complex than small-scale, family-based bands but that are less structured than state societies. They are believed to have been very numerous at various times in the past. Power in chiefdoms is based on kinship relations—how I'm related to you and the other people we live with—and is handed down within families. That sounds a lot like a monarchy, but it's not. A king is the ruler of a state society, and in state societies one's relatives are only one factor in a structure that's based on social classes. State societies, like dynastic Egypt for example, have bureaucracies to collect taxes, centralized armies and legal systems to maintain control, and religions that rationalize the king's right to rule over the poor schlubs on the bottom of the status heap.

It's a matter of degree, of course, but at some point that loose collection of regional chiefs become vassals to a king who rules by divine right. Eventually, at various times in the past, state societies came to dominate much of the world. Everyone reading this (assuming someone *is* reading this…) lives in one state society or another, so the larger significance of Kirch's work is to figure out how we became us.

The Hawaiian Islands are a special case. Way out there in the middle of the Pacific, they weren't settled until about 1,500 years ago. When Europeans arrived in the eighteenth century, Hawaiians had organized themselves into a state society with kings, taxes, monumental architecture, and all the rest. They also had oral histories that recorded decisions the kings and chiefs made, their alliances, and the political backstory you can't get from archaeology. And then there are the accounts of European explorers like Captain James Cook, who visited at the end of the eighteenth century and wrote a lot about the people he met, their customs and politics.

All this makes Hawai'i the only place in the world where there are oral accounts of how a state society came into being ('evolved' if you wish) from chiefdoms. This is pretty exciting stuff because archaeologists' favorite archaic states—dynastic Egypt and the rest—came and went millennia ago and left few or no written records or oral histories—or at least sources that deal with politics. Archaeologists had to reconstruct what these societies were like from analogy. But with Hawai'i there is archaeology *and* the other sources.

We have to start the story with island biogeography, as a lot depends on variations in the local environment. As part of Hawai'i has wet weather and part tends to be dry, people practiced different sorts of agriculture in the different regions. On the wet side they farmed intensively, using all the land as efficiently as they could, and grew a lot of good storable crops like taro,from which *poi* is made. Between circa 1200 and 1500 **CE**, the wet side developed a large population and prospered. They built huge temples, public buildings, and roads. On the dry side it was all about smaller, weaker crops like sweet potatoes and

Making poi by pounding
taro root into paste with
a *pōhaku.*

yams. The people there weren't so well off and didn't have the taro. Their societies had religious rules called *tapu* that were enforced by priests. And one set of rules had to do with the growing of taro. Controlling taro production meant that you controlled part of the relationship between people and the gods. It was part of the way that the kings legitimized themselves as chosen by the gods. So everyone wanted taro.

The islands used to be governed by regional kings, supported by a state religion, an army, taxes, and all the rest. Each island had several kings, and they were constantly at war with each other. Although the rulers on the dry side didn't have the natural resources, they put their wealth into building stronger armies. They wanted to capture the wetlanders' territory to get more productive land and to take over the taro production. Eventually, the drylanders took control, and by the eighteenth century they had turned the weaker rulers into their vassals. King Kamehameha consolidated all these regional rulers and became high king.

As there are oral history and written accounts of the process, archaeologists turned themselves into historical anthropologists by incorporating this information into their interpretations. As Kirch knew quite a bit about the local politics and other events that led up to Kamehameha being in power, he could see the essential role of individual **agency** in moving the process of sociopolitical change along. Without political ambition, there would have been no reason for individuals on the ground to make the decisions that led to this social evolution. To put it another way, the change from chiefdoms to kingdoms was the result of a complex web involving differential regional environmental adaptions and population pressure (some of the long-term causes) and political ambition (the main short-term cause).

The sum up

Neoevolutionary approaches have come a long way since Julian Steward. People like Kirch still want to account for the change from one social form (chiefdom) to another (kingship). However, they don't see it as evolutionary in the usual use of the term. "There is no 'smoking gun,' no universal prime mover," writes Kirch. Rather, chiefdoms are *precursors* to state societies that came about because of a combination of long- and short-term factors.

I've mentioned before that different theoretical approaches and the people who use them don't live in separate realities. Although they generally don't ignore each other's ideas, people who favor neoevolutionary interpretations tend to steer clear of postprocessual ideas. So it's interesting to note that when Kirch writes that kingship required "the manipulation of ideology, notably through daily practice and materialization," he references a 1984 book by Dan Miller and Chris Tilley. This work is considered a cornerstone of postprocessual thought, and is very critical of archaeological practice that is separated from social theory. Kirch's version of neoevolutionary archaeology bridges that gap with style.

The term *tour de force* means something done exceptionally well. A game changer. Pat Kirch's *How Chiefs became Kings* is one of these books, singlehandedly dispelling evolutionary approaches' ancient problem with teleology and determinism. He tackles the 'why things happen' question head-on but is far too immersed in the complex realities to suggest some glib ultimate cause. Instead, Kirch balances short- and long-term influences on outcomes, recognizing that the motives of Great individuals are themselves in part the product of what came before.

Questions to Discuss

What was the racist baggage of the early evolutionists? Can you think of any examples of how it has persisted into modern times?

In what ways is the idea of cultural evolution teleological? And if it is, does that disqualify it as a useful way of looking at change? Why/not?

What does cultural ecology have in common with the Darwinian idea of adaptation?

Is the nature/culture analogy valid? Where does it break down?

Why would anyone care how chiefs became kings? Is it more than just a footnote in the history of the Hawaiian Islands or does it have wider implications? (Author's note: Yes, that's a set-up.)

How do old-timey, ahistorical evolutionary schemes differ from neo-evolutionism in the way they account for change? How does human agency fit into the neoevolutionary way of thinking?

Things to Read

Carson, Rachel
1962 *Silent Spring*. Houghton Mifflin, New York.

Darwin, Charles
1998 *The Origin of Species by means of Natural Selection or the Preservation of Favoured Races in the Struggle for Life*. Reprinted by The Modern Library/Random House, New York.

Hofstadter, Richard
1992 *Social Darwinism in American Thought*. Beacon Press, Boston.

Kirch, Patrick Vinton
2010 *How Chiefs Became Kings: Devine Kingship and the Rise of Archaic States in Ancient Hawai'i*. University of California Press, Berkeley.

Miller, Daniel and Christopher Tilley (Eds.)
1984 Ideology, Power and Prehistory. Cambridge University Press, Cambridge, UK.

Morgan, Lewis Henry
1877 *Ancient Society*. Henry Holt & Company, New York.

Renfrew, Colin
1978 Trajectory, Discontinuity, and Morphogenesis: The Implications of Catastrophe Theory for Archaeology. *American Antiquity* 43:203–222.

Steward, Julian
1977 *Evolution and Ecology*. University of Illinois Press, Chicago.

White, Leslie

1949 *The Science of Culture: A Study of Man and Civilization.*
Grove Press, New York.

CHAPTER 3

MARXISM

The history of all hitherto existing societies
is the history of class struggles.

Karl Marx

What is Marxism?

Marxism is both a theory about how society works and a revolutionary plan for change. It was devised by Karl Marx (1818–1883), which is why he got to put his name on it.[1] Uncle Karl saw the injustices created by nineteenth-century industrialization and developed a **materialist** view of history that emphasized class conflict as the most important force in shaping societies. He can't be ignored or dismissed regardless of your political inclination.

---

1 You'll note that I use "Marxist" not "marxian" in this chapter. The latter is used by people who like Marx's economic analysis but don't care for his revolution.

Archaeological Theory in a Nutshell: Adrian Praetzellis, 41–50.

Margaret Thatcher, Prime Minister of the UK (1979 to 1990), famously said that "there is no such thing as society. There are individual men and women, and there are families." To help the country return to its 'natural' state, Thatcher privatized government functions and effectively took apart Britain's welfare state. People, she said, created their own fate by their own effort. To Thatcher, 'society' and 'class' were merely leftist **ideologies**, not real elements of life.

Marx would have disagreed. He believed that the economic base of society itself determines the ideas that people have about their place in it, not the reverse as claimed by **idealists**. Marx had no patience with middle class intellectuals who sit around in comfy chairs philosophizing about art and ideas, believing that people create society (its economy, political system, religion, and so forth) by moral forces and achieve their place by individual effort. For Marx, the foundation of human society is the way we organize the economic system. All the other aspects of culture and society have emerged from this characteristic.

According to Marx, the driving force in history is conflict between social classes, not some lofty battle between big ideas, charismatic leaders, or religions. By **class** he doesn't mean groups of folk who have certain combinations of wealth, prestige, and education (or the lack thereof) but people who have the same relationship to the **mode of production**—they're either owners or workers. These groups have always had opposing interests: owners want to extract more value from workers, who want the reverse. This is the basis of class conflict and *the* force behind history according to Marxists, some of whom stretch it (in my opinion) to extreme lengths. Philosopher **Jean-Paul Sartre**, for example, went so far as to interpret anti-Semitism as a symbolic representation of the class struggle, claiming that it couldn't exist in a classless society. Tell that to the victims of Stalin's purges in the former Soviet Union, J-P.

Karl Marx (1818–1883) looking to the left, er, right… Marx was born in what is now Germany but was exiled to the UK, where he wrote most of his important works. You can visit his grave in East Highgate Cemetery, London, if you're willing to pay the cemetery's entrance fee. The closest tube station is Archway.

Marxism and archaeology

Many put Marxist archaeologies in the bag labeled **postpro-cessual** approaches. But Marxists view that untidy jumble of ideas as a distraction from the truly important work—creating analyses that will lead to political change. It annoys Marxist archaeologists no end when the writers of textbooks treat their approach as just another postprocessual orientation. "Arg!" they yell (or something like it), "Marx wanted to change the world. He wasn't interested in interpreting history just to satisfy some professor's curiosity and help him get tenure."

This is the hallmark of Marxist archaeology: it is explicitly ideological and focused, utterly rejecting the idea that any interpretation of history or archaeology can ever be value free. Its goals are to reveal the history of class conflict and class consciousness in order to change the political system. It has no interest in developing anthropological generalizations about human behavior. Instead, it focuses on revealing the history of class, putting the issue front and center in much the same way that **feminist** archaeologies do with **gender** relations (see Chapter 6).

Marx claims that class conflict has been going on since antiquity, so it doesn't take a Ph.D. to realize that the evolution of capitalism over the past 500 years makes this a powerful way to see the modern world. Yet, until recent decades its appeal for mainstream archaeologists in North America was muted by: local politics (it wasn't safe to be accused of being a communist), an **empiricism** that mistrusted explanatory models (which I've mentioned in Chapter 1), and the **functionalism** that dominated archaeology and to a large degree still does.

Marxist archaeologists don't just moan about how messed up other societies were; they also look at the class structure of their own discipline. In an important but conveniently ignored article, Randy McGuire and Mark Walker pointed out that the rise of the commercial archaeology (**CRM**) industry and the business-ification of universities has created an archaeological **proletariat**. Itinerant field technicians and adjunct teaching faculty form this cheap pool of temporary labor. These are the working class of the archaeological profession, as opposed to the managers of CRM companies or tenured academics who 'own' their work. Attracted by the carrot of a 'real' job, these folks have little chance of ever achieving it, due, in part, to a university system that creates an oversupply of willing graduates.

The cover of *The Masses* (June 1914), drawn by John Sloan. A miner defends his fallen wife and injured child in this evocative illustration of what became known as the Ludlow Massacre. *The Masses* was a weekly paper that described itself in true Marxist language as "a revolutionary and not a reform magazine."

An example of Marxist archaeology[2]

On April 20, 1914, the Colorado National Guard attacked striking miners and their family members at Ludlow, Colorado. By the end of the day 20 were dead. This was the most infamous event in what came to be known as the Colorado Coal Field War. Most miners were immigrants from Italy, Greece, Eastern Europe, Ireland, Wales, and Mexico. They lived in ethnically mixed settlements where the store, the saloon, and just about every other facility was company-owned. Mining conditions were atrocious—the accident rate was three times the national average.

---

2 The Ludlow Collective, *The Colorado Coal Field War Project* (2003). See McGuire in bibliography at the end of the chapter.

The trouble began in 1913 when the United Mine Workers of America (UMWA) called a strike for higher pay, the right to organize, and to enforce safety regulations. When 90 percent of the miners struck, the company evicted the families, who then moved into a series of tent camps. Ludlow was the largest—its 150 tents housed about 1,200 people. Fearing trouble, the Colorado National Guard had set up a machine gun overlooking Ludlow. And when shots were fired, the Guard opened up on the camp. A second machine gun was added later in the day.

The event has come to be known as the Ludlow Massacre. It is a pivotal incident in American labor history that is still memorialized by the UMWA. The site is a place of pilgrimage.

The Colorado Coal Field War Project was organized as a collective that included Karin Burd, Philip Duke, Amie Gray, Clare Horn, Michael Jacobson, Randall McGuire, Paul Reckner, Dean Saitta, Mark Walker, and Margaret Wood. While some published articles on the topic bear the name of an individual, others are simply authored by the Ludlow Collective. The Collective was intended to be a collaborative effort. In contrast to the competitive, individualistic style of most academic research projects, the Collective's model was cooperation. Data were to be shared within the group instead of being hoarded by some individual until published.

One of the project's goals was to assemble a more complete picture of this event to emphasize working class history and counter the idea of America as a classless society. The remains of burned-out cellars where strikers' families hid from the bullets were uniquely evocative discoveries that speak directly to the tragic history of this place. But the archaeologists also investigated the realities of daily life of workers in the company towns.

One particularly imaginative analysis looks at women's contribution to the development of a class (rather than ethnic) identity on the part of miners and how the mine owners responded to it. Before the strike, miners' wives contributed to the household income by taking in boarders. This practice can be seen in the archaeological record by the high proportion of tin cans (canned food was expensive) and large cooking and serving vessels. Good for the miners, but not for the owners since—according to the Collective's Margaret Wood—communal living solidified social ties and contributed to class consciousness. Following the strike, the owners made it more difficult for families to take in boarders. This both made miners more dependent on their wages and, most importantly, encouraged each family to *privatize* its interest. The trend away from corporate households can be seen in a dramatic decrease in large food preparation vessels and a concurrent increase in canning artifacts and the bones of wild and home-raised animals, as women tried to adapt to the new conditions.

Archaeologists tend to relegate women to the role of reinforcers of the status quo whose social pretensions are supposedly revealed in their consumer practices: they buy fancy artifacts to advance their family's social status. A Marxist approach turns this idea on its head. The Collective challenges the assumption that everyone aspired to the middle class and modeled themselves after middle class ideals.

Ludlow's workers included African Americans, White Americans, and people from a variety of European immigrant groups. Each group had its own interests, played off against each other, and participated in an ethnically based hierarchy of sorts. Faced with this undeniable reality, many archaeologists would have chosen to emphasize ethnicity in their interpretation. Not so the Collective. Drawing on Marxist principles, they posited that the common experience of daily life was class-based and crosscut ethnicity. The Ludlow Collective's class-oriented approach turned what could have been a **normative** study of subsistence and cultural conformity into an interpretation that tackles issues relevant to the place and time.

The sum up

One critique of Marxist archaeology (and one that Margaret Thatcher would agree with) is that it's **deterministic**. That is, even before the first trowel hits the dirt the archaeologist assumes that class struggle was behind whatever went on at the site.

It is certainly true that classic structural Marxism identifies economics as the prime mover *a priori* regardless of circumstances, leaving human beings as impotent actors in circumstances over which they have no control (see Chapter 10). The Ludlow study shows that Marxist archaeologists don't dismiss out of hand every influence other than economics. They do consider ethnicity and gender, although ultimately both of these tend to serve an economic interpretation. "Men make their own history," wrote Uncle Karl, "but they do not make it in circumstances chosen by themselves." It's not that individuals have no **agency,** but that the class-dominated situation in which they live in limits their effectiveness in carrying it out.

Perhaps the most distinctive aspect of this example of Marxist-influenced archaeology is the application of Marx's insights in everyday practice—including the archaeologists' professional practices. By creating a cooperative model for research the Ludlow Collective tried to avoid creating the very hierarchical structure that Marx abhorred.

Questions to Discuss

Why is Marxism such a powerful collection of ideas for understanding the past? Must you be a believing communist or socialist to use Marx's ideas?

To what degree is Marxism teleological? Is that one of its strengths? Is Marxist analysis only relevant to societies that have social classes? How would you use Marxist analysis to look at a relatively egalitarian group, such as a hunter-gatherer-forager society?

With its strong emphasis on class and group action, do the people of the past get lost in Marxist archaeology? How might a Marxist archaeologist respond to this critique?

Things to Read

Childe, V. Gordon

1942 *What Happened in History?* Penguin Books, Harmondsworth, UK.

McGuire, Randy

2002 *A Marxist Archaeology.* Percheron Press, New York.

McGuire, Randall and Mark Walker

1999 Class Confrontations in Archaeology. *Historical Archaeology 33*(1):159–183.

McGuire, Randall and Paul Reckner (For the Ludlow Collective)

2003 Building a Working-Class Archaeology: The Colorado Coal Field War Project. *Industrial Archaeology Review. 15*(2):84–95.

Patterson, Thomas

2003 *Marx's Ghost: Conversations with Archaeologists.* Berg, Oxford, UK.

Sartre, Jean-Paul

1985 *Anti-semite and Jew.* Schocken Books, New York.

Thatcher, Margaret

1987 Interview with Margaret Thatcher by Douglas Keay. *Woman's Own* October 31, 1987.

CHAPTER 4

CRITICAL THEORY

Ideology is the imaginary relationship of individuals to the real conditions of their existence.

Louis Althusser

What is critical theory?

Critical theory is a practice that uses insights from the social sciences, philosophy, and the humanities to critique contemporary and past societies.

Many people (philosophers in particular) who might say they 'do' critical theory base their practice in Karl Marx's ideas about how groups construct and use **ideology** to maintain their power over others (see Chapter 3). Uncle Karl, you may recall, pointed out that people essentially trick themselves into not seeing the power relations that structure their lives by developing a **false consciousness**. Mechanisms like religion, he said, legitimatize the way a particular society operates by making its cultural norms seem like the only right way to live.

Archaeological Theory in a Nutshell: Adrian Praetzellis, 51–60.

Marx noted all this and moved on. He knew that ideology was an important force, but he was more concerned with its results than how it worked. That wasn't enough for **Louis Althusser** (1918–1990). Growing up with the horrific results of Nazi Germany's fascist ideology around him, Althusser took Marx's notion and ran with it. He emphasized that ideology is an active force in society that works because it is injected into daily practices and conventional patterns of behavior. Most importantly, he pointed out that ideology becomes part of our experience of reality. We do not question it because its logic is 'obvious' and self-evidently rational. We take it for granted.

Althusser was interested in the institutions that societies set up to enforce and reinforce their ideologies. These include

Louis Althusser (1918–1990). An important voice in what is now critical theory, he was interested in the role of ideology and the cult of personality in social reproduction.

repressive apparatuses like the legal system, as well as religion, education, and the mass media, whose control is more furtive. This model of impersonal structures and institutions was fine as far as it went, but how ideology quite worked on the ground was still a little fuzzy.

Sitting in his prison cell (he'd been arrested by the Italian fascist leader Benito Mussolini), **Antonio Gramsci** (1891–1937) had both the time and good cause to think about these matters. He reasoned that even the dimmest specimens of humankind would, in time, uncover the kind of static system proposed by Althusser. Instead, Gramsci presented ideology as a highly dynamic *process*, a battle whose weapons were constantly changing and, therefore, more difficult to penetrate. Social classes, said Gramsci, are perpetually competing with each other for domination using a subtle system of ideological symbols. Seen in this way, a successful ideology is all pervasive consciousness or cultural **hegemony**.

What exactly did these guys mean by ideology? Well, any set of assumptions about the world that seem so self-evident that they don't require any thought or critical analysis can be part of an ideology. The medieval **Great Chain of Being**, for example, is the expression of an ideology about the hierarchical relationship between all the elements of creation, from rocks to angels. It purports to show that the relationship between social classes was established by God. If you accept this ideology, social change is impossible and to attempt it (by revolution, for example) is wrong because that would contravene the natural order of things.

Hegemonic ideology works because it is constantly being reinforced by sets of conventional behaviors and the material symbols associated with them. In nineteenth-century America, for example, upper middle class women were considered by their society (and often considered themselves) to be appendages to their husbands, whose job it was to protect these weak, decorative creatures from the world's harsh realities. This ideology was expressed to others by decorating one's home with artifacts that were considered 'appropriate' and tasteful.[1]

Material culture plays an essential part in this game. And wherever you find material culture, you'll find a postprocessual archaeologist ready to tell you what it means.

Critical theory and archaeology

Exposing hegemonic ideologies that support the power elite is vital to a critical analysis. Archaeologists do it with material culture by revealing the **recursive** power of artifacts. Objects don't just passively reflect the values of the groups that use them. They actively work to create and reinforce these values.

One of the best-known examples of the power of artifacts to influence ideology is Mark Leone's interpretation of the garden of William Paca, an eighteenth-century Maryland aristocrat. His prestige in decline, Paca built a complex formal garden using the rules of perspective and optical illusion. He created a series of terraces and symmetrical garden beds that imposed order on the landscape. According to Leone, the end result was a not-too-subtle demonstration to Paca's guests that the great man was deep and sophisticated, had control over the laws of nature, and, consequently, that his illustrious position was deserved and 'natural.'

Followers of critical theory in historical archaeology focus on uncovering the origins of ideologies that rationalized racism, sexism, and classism. Although no one will be too surprised to learn that they place capitalism at the root of these ideologies, theirs is not a philosophy of unmitigated gloom—for where the dominant ideology demands control, people resist! And part of the critical theorists' goal is to document that process and present it to descendant groups. Critical theorists carry out their agenda in much the same way as Marxists, through practical engagement with groups that historically experienced (and

---

1 Edith Wharton's 1913 novel, *The Custom of the Country*, is a brilliant description of this way of life.

continue to experience) repression and exploitation, notably ethnic minorities and the working class.

If ideology had these effects in the past, then it surely is doing the same today. Contemporary archaeologists pursue research and create interpretations that support (or at least aren't too objectionable to) the institutions that nourish their work and advance their careers. However, critical theorists who work at universities may find themselves unemployed when they direct their analyses too pointedly at their own institutions. They walk a perilous path for, like Marxists, critical theorists hope to inspire social change and a more equitable society.

Which is exactly what the next section is about.

An example of critical theory–inspired archaeology[2]

Newspaper columnist Judith "Miss Manners" Martin is an authority on correct social behavior. She takes a humanitarian view of the purpose of etiquette: the rules exist to help people get along amicably in situations that might otherwise be awkward. This pleasant vision is born of a desire to see human motivation in its most innocuous light, and I would like to think it's true. In eighteenth-century Maryland, however, things appear to have been quite different.

Paul Shackel's work focused on the same issue as his colleague Mark Leone: the way in which Maryland's power elite (such as the gardening William Paca) legitimized and maintained their authority. Shackel argued that competing segments of Maryland society used an ever increasing and more complicated array of artifacts as part of their strategy to achieve and keep their power. The attentive reader will recall that Gramsci had something to say on this topic: that individuals with the same interest form associations to improve their access to power, developing ideologies that support their hegemony. Shackel wants to see how this worked on the ground—how these groups used material culture to make their right to power appear 'natural.'

---

2 Paul Shackel, *Personal Discipline and Material Culture* (1993).

Shackel was concerned with the most mundane of objects: clocks, dinner forks, and ceramic serving vessels, among other things. But Shackel believed that boring is in the eye of the beholder, that these artifacts have no fixed symbolic meaning and can only be understood by considering the **context** in which they were used. So what *did* they mean to the people who used them and those who observed them in others' parlors? For the answer to this we must consider the history of table manners.

Mealtime in most seventeenth-century Euro-American homes was a truly communal activity that involved a lot of grabbing from communal bowls of food. Your plate or wooden trencher sat in front of you, and if you were lucky enough to have multiple courses, you ate them all from the same vessel. Knives and spoons were similarly up for grabs, and the rules that governed their use, such as they were, could be quickly figured out by just watching other people.

Shackel looked at archaeological collections from several points in the eighteenth and nineteenth centuries and showed that the complexity of dining services increased dramatically over the years. This was reflected in greater numbers and sizes of plates, the variety of functions they represented, as well as a tendency toward matching sets. And here's the point: *increasing complexity involved a more intricate system of rules to govern the system,* and etiquette books proliferated. Practices acceptable to your grandparents were now looked on with contempt.

It was clear to Shackel that the eighteenth-century dining room was an important venue of ideological competition. Here the rules of etiquette could be used to draw a bright line between those in the know (who belonged) and those weren't (and who didn't). Furthermore, the ever-increasing variety of consumer goods made it possible to change the rules by bringing in new pieces of technology, such as dining forks and plates whose size indicated their role in the game. The rules of polite dining were a moving target. The aspiring middle class learned one set of exacting behaviors only to find that it had been superseded by another invented by their social superiors. The middle

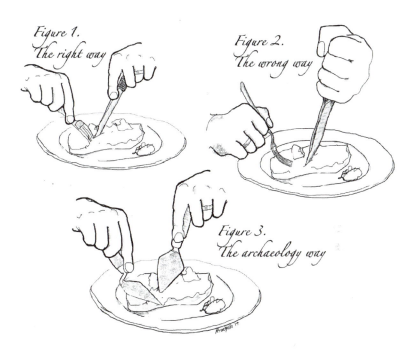

Figure 1.
The right way

Figure 2.
The wrong way

Figure 3.
The archaeology way

Table manners. Social groups differentiate themselves by means of symbolic behaviors. Elite social classes have long used their knowledge of the complex and changing rules of etiquette to sort out those who belong and those who don't. (Archaeologists hardly ever eat with trowels, by the way.)

class purchased consumer 'must haves' only to discover that the elite had long ago moved on to something rarer and, consequently, more desirable.

The political landscape of eighteenth-century Maryland was quite unstable. Wealth and power were moving from the hands of planters and craftsmen to urban merchants and the holders of capital. From those with old money and deep roots in legitimized power to those who had not yet authenticated their position. These groups fought with symbolic weapons—artifacts and the rules that surrounded them—to exclude and to justify exclusion, to include and legitimize. A man who knew how to navigate the dining table signaled that he belonged in sophisticated society and had the natural fitness to govern.

The sum up

The symbolic approach relies heavily on documentary records to provide the necessary context for interpretation. However, as we have seen before, archaeology often makes its contribution by showing how historical processes worked out on the ground, in particular places, at specific times, and in the lives of real people—and how material culture contributed to it all. Some of the patterns noted by Shackel and Leone were formerly recognized by Jim Deetz, who developed an apolitical, cultural model of change to account for them (see Chapter 8). Deetz was interested in showing how artifacts reflected changes in American culture. The critical theorists injected class and power into the situation and revealed the force behind the changes that Deetz observed: mercantile capitalism.

As practiced by archaeologists, critical theory is sometimes as much about praxis as it is an approach to understanding. As advocates for social change, practitioners are concerned with creating a useable history for disenfranchised descendant communities. Since most people are more attracted by stories that are relevant to their own experience than to academic generalizations, archaeologists like Parker Potter, another Leone associate, put a great deal of effort into investigating issues that descendant groups find important. Potter's book, *Public Archaeology in Annapolis,* is a great example of this practice. In fact it's more about the process of doing archaeology than what the archaeology means. The result is quite introspective and demonstrates that its practitioners care a great deal about the outcomes of their work.

The demise of the Soviet Union and the transformation of other communist countries into wide open capitalist economies has led some social theorists and even more politicians to dismiss Marx's **historical materialism** as a discredited model of how the world works. As critical theory relies less on historical materialism than on the role of ideology, it may be the alternative for those who don't want to throw out the baby with the bathwater.

Questions to Discuss

What would an apolitical interpretation of history look like?

If archaeological interpretation is unavoidably political, how can the archaeologist maintain a multivocal perspective? Doesn't someone end up being right and someone wrong?

If these concepts are applicable to the past and to other people, why don't academic archaeologists apply them to themselves and their profession? What might they discover if they did?

Think up some examples of modern artifacts that are tools of various political ideologies on the left *and* on the right sides of the political spectrum.

Things to Read

Althusser, Louis.

1984 *Althusser: A Critical Reader.* Edited by Gregory Elliott. Blackwell Press, Cambridge, Massachusetts.

Deetz, James F.

1996 *In Small Things Forgotten: An Archaeology of Early American Life.* Anchor Books, New York.

Gramsci, Antonio

1971 *Selections from The Prison Notebooks.* Edited by Quentin Hoare and Geoffrey Smith. International, New York.

Leone, Mark

1984 Interpreting Ideology in Historical Archaeology: Using the Rules of Perspective in the William Paca Garden in Annapolis, Maryland. In Daniel Miller and Chris Tilley (Eds.), *Ideology, Power and Prehistory* (pp. 25–35). Cambridge University Press, Cambridge, UK.

Leone, Mark

1987 Towards a Critical Archaeology. *Current Anthropology* 28:283–302.

Miller, Daniel and Christopher Tilley (Eds.)

1984 *Ideology, Power and Prehistory.* Cambridge University Press, Cambridge, UK.

Potter, Parker

1994 *Public Archaeology in Annapolis: A Critical Approach to History in Maryland's Ancient City.* Smithsonian Institution Press, Washington, D.C.

Shackel, Paul

1993 *Personal Discipline and Material Culture: An Archaeology of Annapolis, Maryland, 1695–1870.* University of Tennessee Press, Knoxville.

CHAPTER 5
POSTCOLONALISM

*Postcards and postcolonialism are two things I advocate
for people who can't afford to go on vacation.*

Bauvard

What is postcolonialism?

Postcolonialism is an approach to history and culture that
emphasizes the aftermath of colonialism. From the sixteenth
through the twentieth centuries, a few great powers (mostly European) controlled most of the globe. The histories they
wrote were of great men doing great things in war, politics,
and commerce. Rule Britannia, Manifest Destiny, and the rest.
But suppose we look at colonialism from the other side, from
the perspective of the indigenous peoples and how the process
affected the culture of the colonizers themselves...

Things seem rather different now, don't they?

People have been writing about the effects of imperialism
for a long time, and some of the most important ideas have

Archaeological Theory in a Nutshell: Adrian Praetzellis, 61–72.

come from non-Western nations. A lot of this scholarship is overtly political and, not surprisingly, even anti-Western. The concept of **orientalism,** for example, was devised by Palestinian American **Edward Said** to describe how colonial powers justify their imperialist schemes by presenting non-Western peoples as barely human. Western scholarship in general and anthropologists in particular are said to contribute to this way of thinking by creating one dimensional representations of non-Western societies. Think of how American Indians are often portrayed as a group that was originally noble but is now degenerate, and with a reverence for nature that emerges from their animal-like closeness to it. This was the type of thinking that lead to the forced removal of Native American and Australian Aboriginal children to remote schools where the remnants of their purportedly irrational cultures could be replaced by sensible Western ways of thinking.

In a sort of extreme ethnocentrism, the colonizer's culture and institutions are taken as a touchstone, while those of the colonized **Other** are discounted. In fact, that very word **Other** is part of the postcolonial vocabulary, borrowed from French (!) psychoanalyst Jacques Lacan, who used it to define the relationship of the individual to someone else: me and you. It doesn't take much imagination to analogize this to groups of people: us and them.

It's clear that colonization is not just about one country dominating another by military might. Of course, an army is pretty much essential for back-up. But as everyone from **Antonio Gramsci** to the imperial Roman emperors knew, it's a lot more efficient to change the culture of colonized people than to continually imprison or slaughter large numbers of them to get them to toe the line. Less expensive, too. If you can get the 'natives' to adopt ways of thinking that support your new economic and legal structures, you've got yourself a self-policing society. British imperialists in India used this strategy very effectively. How else could a tiny nation dominate one of the most populous regions on earth? Instead of replacing India's traditional rulers,

Commemorative plate celebrating Queen Victoria's 50 years on the British throne. Victoria was the symbolic head of an empire that controlled almost one-quarter of the world's land mass and one-fifth of its population.
(From the author's collection.)

they assimilated them. Instead of using British soldiers to police the continent, they developed indigenous regiments of intensely loyal Sikhs and Ghurkas.

That old ex-con and hero of Chapter 4 (critical theory) Gramsci came up with the term **subaltern** to mean a politically uncoordinated mass of people. Scholars in India took this idea to develop histories of colonized peoples as an alternative to the tales told by the colonial power. Writing about colonized

Asians, **Gayatri Spivak** famously asked: "Can the subaltern speak?" In other words, can a group that was effaced from traditional history be resurrected and gain a voice?

Enter the archaeologists...

Postcolonialism and archaeology

Sprivak's subalterns sound a lot like those Ruth Tringham described as **faceless blobs**—people who are left out of conventional accounts of history and life. Modern archaeologists include in this group women, enslaved people, and ethnic and sexual minorities. In postcolonial archaeology they are often Native Americans and other indigenous people. And to these we can add some settlers who, although part of the colonialization effort, were themselves on the social margins.

But before we start getting too smug, it's worth remembering that archaeology itself contributed to the colonial project. The Indiana Jones-like character who plundered (such a judgmental word) colonized nations for nifty artifacts isn't entirely a fictional image. The great museums of most European capitals are full of other countries' patrimony. The case of the Elgin Marbles (aka, the Parthenon Marbles) comes to mind. These 2,500-year-old sculptures were cut from the Parthenon in Athens and purchased by a British lord who gave them to the British Museum. Greece wants them back, by the way.

For many years archaeologists advocated (or at least didn't oppose) the view that pre-colonized peoples lived in a sort of timeless and unchanging culture, and that it took the influence of the colonizers to help them 'advance.' It was unthinkable that indigenous Africans were building engineering marvels like Great Zimbabwe when the settlers' ancestors were living in mud huts. So archaeologists came up with some ingenious workarounds to rationalize their erroneous views. Indigenous archaeology, wherein descendants take on the role of archaeologist, is an outcome of our discipline misrepresenting or ignoring descendants' views.

In recent years, archaeologists have often taken the meeting of indigenous peoples and settlers as an opportunity to study culture contact. What happens when a modern society meets a traditional one? Archaeologist David Hurst Thomas called his three volume series *Columbian Consequences* to emphasize that there were important cultural outcomes from Spanish settlement in North America, not just from the more studied British colonial system.

Although colonial authorities try their best, the domination process is never complete. Total assimilation is rarely achieved in the short term, and the cultural forms that emerge from colonization are not quite what the colonizers had in mind. Both sides are changed in unpredictable ways, and new identities are formed. The new social identities that emerged on colonial frontiers from South Africa to New Zealand were not fixed and unchanging—just the reverse. So archaeologists use *process* terms like **ethnogenesis** to describe how these hybrid cultures came into being and evolved.

Archaeologists frequently work on sites where the residents' stories were untold because they were overshadowed by the historic events that took place there. Their efforts advance archaeology's humanistic goal of enabling at least some representatives of the subaltern classes to speak or, at least, to be represented.

An example of postcolonial archaeology[1]

The year was 1776, and while certain revolutionary events were unfolding in faraway Philadelphia, a group of soldiers, their families, and miscellaneous hangers-on set up camp on a windy headland overlooking San Francisco Bay. The government of Spain had a rather tenuous control over northern California and hoped that this outpost would discourage other colonial powers from taking a bite. They also expected it be the first of many

---

1 Barbara Voss, *The Archaeology of Ethnogenesis* (2008).

settlements that would populate this wild northern frontier with Spanish citizens and their dependents.

The military presence at El Presidio de San Francisco numbered 30–40 officers and soldiers, but women and children brought the population to about 200. El Presidio was not just a camp of soldiers but a complete community. Its social structure was dominated by the military hierarchy and the Spanish colonial *sistema de castas* that divided people into as many as 40 groups, each defined by its perceived racial character and each with its own role and responsibilities in the little society. The system was designed to maintain the status quo and prevent undesirable social mobility. However, archaeologist Barb Voss shows how even within this apparently rigid structure some

Mestizo (Anonymous 1770). The colonial Spanish government carefully distinguished between many grades of *castas* (persons of mixed 'race') based on the degree of heritage of one's ancestors. A *mestiza/mestizo* was defined as the child of Spanish and Indigenous parents.

individuals' *casta* status changed over time between *español, mestizo, mulato,* and *indio,* the principal castes. And from these changes developed a new cultural identity: *Californio.* This is ethnogenesis, "the birthing," says Voss, "of new cultural identities."

Directives from Spain established, at least in theory, the physical and social structure of El Presidio. The archaeology shows how people adapted these rules to local conditions and their own desires. Presidio authorities responded by manipulating the physical structure to combat these insidious cultural changes.

Physical changes in El Presidio's architecture show this response, as interpreted by archaeologist Voss. It is well known that the quadrangle formed by El Presidio's curtain wall was expanded by 220 percent in 1815. Most scholars would interpret this expansion on face value as a purely utilitarian event. But Voss has another idea. Pointing out that El Presidio was a mishmash of buildings and structures at this time, she suggests that if functionality had been the goal, the authorities would simply have tacked buildings onto the outside of the curtain wall. But they didn't.

Instead, says she, the leadership's real goal was to create a larger enclosed space where everyday activities would be centralized and made more or less public. Reducing private space transfered activities away from the household—perhaps the most important locus of ethnogenesis—to public space where they could be monitored by the increasingly paternalistic military command. In other words, forcing people into the open discourages transgressive behavior. As the public façade of the outpost, Voss suggests that the plaza was designed to project a controlled environment reflected in homogeneous architecture and gendered social practices as an "image of ethnic respectability" in which each and everyone is behaving appropriately in relation to his or her respective *casta.*

In pits excavated for clay adjacent to the curtain wall, archaeologists found rich collections of artifacts discarded as refuse. Yet very few of these were Native American objects. This contrasts.with the situation in nearby Tennessee Hollow—a residential area downhill and out of sight of the plaza—where colonial and Native American artifacts were found together. This material segregation, says Voss, reflects the social segregation within the post itself.

The archaeologists' analysis of nearly 7,500 ceramic sherds from a refuse deposit created, presumably, by Presidio households shows half a dozen ware types from Faience to Mexican *galera*. Instead of taking the usual approach and assuming that *ware type* is the way to understand status and gender at El Presidio, Voss emphasizes the vessels' forms and functions. She concludes that "different ware types were functionally integrated to complete the colonial table," evoking a functionally and aesthetically diverse table setting that mirrored the heterogeneous society that created it.

El Presidio was the site of complex cultural transformations. Its story is not only of international power politics, conquest, and matters military, but of how people subverted an apparently rigid social structure for their own purposes, and the official response. Through her close study of documentary and archaeological evidence, Barb Voss reveals that the colonizers themselves were transformed by their experience. Her emphasis on everyday interactions and things taken for granted shows us what was behind the raw coercive power that we usually think of as the foundation of colonialism.

The sum up

Jim Deetz's idea of the scope of historical archaeology was European cultures' "impact on and interaction with the cultures of indigenous peoples." The postcolonial project expands this idea. It does not assume that cultural change was unilinear (a straight line from the traditional to the modern) or unidirectional (from the colonizer to the colonized). Or that members of the subaltern classes were powerless or ignorant of their own interest. Postcolonial analysis even suggests that instead of being merely the passive recipients of colonial 'impact,' colonized people were well aware of their situation and even used it to get what they wanted (see Chapter 9).

But wait. What's that I hear? It's a whole room full of postcolonial types banging their shoes on the table. Let's not get sentimental, they insist. The colonizers did whatever was necessary to achieve economic and ideological domination, and played havoc with traditional societies. Who remembers that millions of Indians died in the famines of the 1860s and 1870s because of British East India Company policies?

Like **postmodernism, poststructuralism**, and any number of concepts to which some deep thinker has added the *post-*prefix, the idea of postcolonialism is to take an entirely different orientation to something about which we were formerly comfortable in our understanding. If we think of places like El Presidio de San Francisco merely as army camps concerned with military matters, we miss half of their meaning.

Archaeology participates in the postcolonial project, in part, by returning some dignity to a few of colonialism's subjects. But in our desire to humanize and empower we must not forget the conditions under which they lived.

Questions to Discuss

Is postcolonialism a legitimate research agenda or a politically cor-rect litany of complaints and sour grapes about things that hap-pened a long time ago? (Author's note: That phrasing is meant to stimulate discussion. Please don't picket my office.)

What was it about nineteenth-century cultural anthropology that made its results so easy to hijack to support the colonizers' schemes? Could these scholars have prevented their work from being misused? How?

Identify some groups that could be considered Other in modern Western society. What do they have in common?

How might postcolonial theory be useful to a new nation state that is developing its national identity? How might archaeology contribute to this effort?

Things to Read

Deetz, James F.
1996 *In Small Things Forgotten: An Archaeology of Early American Life.* Anchor Books, New York.

Lacan, Jaques
1977 *Écrits: A Selection.* Translated by Alan Sheridan. Norton Books, New York.

Moxham, Roy
2001 *The Great Hedge of India.* Carroll & Graf, New York.

Said, Edward
1979 *Orientalism.* Vintage Books, New York.

Silverberg, Robert
1968 *Mound Builders of Ancient America.* New York Graphic Society, Greenwich, Connecticut.

Spivak, Gayatri Chakravorty
1988 Can the subaltern speak? In Cary Nelson and Lawrence Grossberg (Eds.), *Marxism and the Interpretation of Culture* (pp. 271–313). Macmillan Education, Basingstoke, UK.

Thomas, David Hurst (Ed.)
1989 *Columbian Consequences.* Smithsonian Institution Press, Washington, D.C.

Tringham, Ruth
1991 Households with Faces: the Challenge of Gender in Prehistoric Architectural Remains. In Joan Gero and Margaret (Eds.), *Engendering Archaeology: Women in Prehistory* (pp. 93–131). Basil Blackwell, Cambridge, Massachusetts.

Voss, Barbara L.

2008 *The Archaeology of Ethnogenesis.* University of California Press, Berkeley.

CHAPTER 6

FEMINISM

The first problem for all of us, men and women,
is not to learn but to unlearn.

Gloria Steinem

What is feminism?

Feminism is a rowdy assemblage of ideas whose goal is to understand and advance the lives of women. The much bumperstickered "Feminism is the radical notion that women are people" (attributed to Cheris Kramerae) captures the idea that we can't separate the movement's intellectual content from its goal of social change. Non-political feminism is an oxymoron.

Mary Wollstonecraft, whose daughter would write the horror novel *Frankenstein*, created a furor by suggesting in *A Vindication of the Rights of Women* (1792) that:

- men and women are moral and intellectual equals
- girls should have an academically challenging education, and
- women should be allowed to work outside the home

Archaeological Theory in a Nutshell: Adrian Praetzellis, 73–83.

·Unthinkable!

Wollstonecraft and other **first wave** feminists made slow advances in areas of basic social equality, such as liberalized divorce and the right of married women to their own property. Voting had to wait until 1893 (New Zealand). No doubt Saudi Arabia will catch on eventually.

The first generation of feminists focused on reforming society in general through good works—improving living conditions for the underclass, educational reform, and temperance. So-called **second wave** feminism, aka the women's liberation movement, wanted to advance women in society. Sparked by the anti-war and civil rights movements of the 1960s, books such as Kate Millett's *Sexual Politics* (1970) began to form feminism's intellectual underpinnings, while Germaine Greer's wildly successful *The Female Eunuch* (1971) brought feminism into the mainstream. The movement wanted to reveal the entrenched sexist bias in Western culture and to undermine the era's taken-for-granted, androcentric values that restrict women's roles in society. Among its goals were reproductive control for women and equity between men and women in the workplace.

The feminism that emerged in the 1980s and 1990s was shaped by intellectual concerns. Compared with the focused, practical goals of earlier eras, **third wave** feminism (which is where we are now according to Rebecca Walker, and she should know) is a diverse, rather academic, and theory-heavy movement whose practitioners may take a variety of approaches, from **postcolonialism** to **queer theory** (see Chapters 5 and 7, respectively). Scholars like bell hooks (no, her name doesn't have capitals) in *Ain't I a Woman?* (1981) re-focused the movement by pointing out that the second wave had screwed up by assuming that the experiences of white, heterosexual, middle class women reflected all women. Although the arrival of pop culture 'post-feminists' like Camille Paglia has made the scene both increasingly grumpy and tough to pin down, many third wave feminists believe that ways of seeing the past and reshaping the future should reflect the fact that females and males are equally valuable.

Feminist theorists Mary Wollstonecraft (*left*) and Rebecca Walker (*right*) of the eighteenth and twenty-first centuries, respectively. The graffiti artist and her subject represent practical activism and resistance to injustice.

Feminism and archaeology

Consider these two scenarios:

First, there's the old fashioned and now discredited view of

Man the Hunter

who fought the natural elements and faced the dangers of the wild world to kill and bring home meat. Exhausted, he rested as the women of the cave cleaned and processed his bloody prize.

75

And then there's

Man the Archaeologist

who labors in the sun (or rain) hacking at the ground, extracting precious objects that he brings to the lab. Exhausted, he rests as the women of the dig clean and process his dirt-encrusted discoveries.

Any kind of parallel there? Hmm, let me see now...

Until fairly recently, women in our field were all too often assigned what Joan Gero called "archaeological housework." While they worked in the lab, cleaning and sorting artifacts, men went out digging and eventually published the results of the work. And the writers of these excavation reports interpreted 'their' discoveries in a similarly androcentric way, reproducing the same gender roles in their writing as they experienced in their lives as men. Women were assumed to be passive, subservient, and home-bound. Men were active, dominant, and in charge of outside relations. In short, while women stayed home taking care of the domestic details, men were out making history and, in the case of archaeologists, publishing it as well.

Clearly, a feminist archaeology would have to focus on **gender** roles in the present as well as the past, and scholars began to expose this all-too-obvious flaw in both their thought processes and practice. In an early example, the authors in Frances Dahlberg's book, *Woman the Gatherer* (1981), showed how common stereotypes falsely conflated biological sex with socially ascribed gender roles and how they had caused women to be effectively written out of prehistory. When the 1989 Chacmool Conference focused on gender, things were off and running. A couple of years later in 1991 two important volumes were published that put a feminist archaeology of gender on the map: Conkey and Gero's *Engendering Archaeology* and Donna Seifert's *Gender in Historical Archaeology*. The latter includes studies of Native American women, gender relations in a logging camp, and prostitutes. People like Whitney Battle-Baptiste and Barbara Voss represent third wave feminism in their black feminist and sexual minority perspectives, respectively (see Chapter 6).

An example of feminist archaeology[1]

Janet Spector was frustrated. Little Rapids was a fabulous archaeological site, but to fall into the time-honored way of describing it would miss so much. Then student archaeologist Joan Junquiera found the object that would set Spector on a new route to interpreting the site and the people who lived there—it was a decorated bone awl handle.

Little Rapids (*Iyan Ceyaka Atonwan* in the Dakota language) was an 1830s–40s Wahpeton Dakota settlement on the Minnesota River near what is now Minneapolis. It was a summer village devoted to planting, tending, and harvesting corn, the main Wahpeton crop. Visiting fur traders, US government officials, anthropologists, and missionaries left a rich documentary record of this group that, like all historic records, says as much about the people who wrote it as those they described.

Archaeologists had visited the site before Spector arrived in the summer of 1980, but since this was the first Wahpeton Dakota village to be formally excavated, she had to go to nearby Fort Michilimackinac to see comparative artifacts. In the usual way of things, archaeologists at the fort had written a shelf of technical reports on their discoveries, carefully documenting everything and classifying the artifacts into a branching root-like array of types, sub-types, and varieties. It was all very scientific and, as far as they were concerned, fulfilled their primary professional responsibility: to make their data accessible to others. And yet...

With boxes of artifacts from her work at the site waiting to be interpreted, Spector had to decide just how she would present the Little Rapids story. There was the traditional approach

---

1 Janet Spector, *What This Awl Means* (1993).

77

to consider: This would involve classifying the objects by type and variety, and assigning each one a place in some functional scheme. The awl handle, for example, could be thought of as 'Type I, Variety (a)' according to the scheme devised by the archaeologists at Michilimackinac. Next, the awl handle would be tabulated along with like items and discussed under a category such as "Household Context of Utilization—Maintenance and Repair." She could have taken this approach and that would be that.

Spector knew that she was faced with one of paradoxes of archaeological practice: we must classify artifacts to understand them, yet this very process limits our ability to interpret what the objects might have meant to the people who used them. In this case, the seemingly neutral "maintenance and repair" category in fact carries with it unstated assumptions about the role of women as mere support players on the stage of Dakota life. In a skillful use of historic accounts and oral history, Spector showed that the awl's incised dots and lines are public records of its owner's accomplishments, similar to public displays created by the group's men.

A bone-handled awl of the type found at the Little Rapids site on the Minnesota River. Awls were and are used to pierce leather and in basket making. A traditional Dakota woman would decorate and personalize her awl.

Taken from this perspective the awl is a lot more than just a punch for making holes in leather.

At this point the archaeologist left conventional practice far behind her. Instead of discussing the site in standard divisions of history, structure, and content, she offers a narrative of how the awl may have been lost and the object's meaning to the woman who owned it in the context of 1830s Dakota life. The fact that much of the action cannot be documented in the usual way doesn't distract from the insights that she offers. It *is* a story (albeit a well-documented one), and the reader is fully aware of the fact. Equally important, Spector talks about objects in the archaeological context of their discovery rather than as one of a number of functionally similar objects found throughout the site. Since the awl was found in a refuse pit, Spector asks how it got there and what might be its relation to the pit's other contents. In this way, we get to see the artifacts not merely as chunks of technology that, divorced from the culture that used them, can be understood by the scientist's technical analyses. Instead, they are presented as objects that functioned together in a living community.

Dakota society has been described as dominated by hunting, a male activity. Yet it was women who sowed, tended, and harvested the corn that was the focus of Little Rapids. Dakota women believed it positively inappropriate for their men to help with these tasks, so strict were the group's gender divisions. Thus, Spector showed that the large, artifact-rich storage pits her crew uncovered—elements of the archaeological structure of the site itself—are more part of the women's world than of the men's.

There are other good examples of feminist archaeology out there, but Spector's *Awl* is fabulous. To say just that it's good feminist archaeology would be to minimize the work's significance. It is simply good archaeology.

The sum up

Most archaeologists have not been particularly quick to see what feminism has to do with them. It's tacitly understood in historical archaeology that women purchased most of the things we find, from the remains of meals in the form of animal bones to the ubiquitous sherds of ceramic dinnerware. And many archaeologists now try to spot the archaeological signatures of women on their sites and in the artifacts they dig up. Yet identifying the archaeological evidence of women is merely what archaeologists should be doing as a matter of course.

That men and women lived together in the past will not be much of a surprise to anyone. A feminist archaeology does not just provide archaeological examples of this historical fact—what's called the 'add women and stir' approach. We know that gender relations existed; the question is how did they function at particular places and times in the past?

The central characteristic of feminist archaeology is that it is 'gendered.' That is, it recognizes that gender relations is and always has been one of the main organizing principals of human society. Thus, its goals will continue to be exposing and undermining andocentrism as well as emphasizing women's **agency** in creating their own lives and their societies.

Questions to Discuss

Is 'gender' really that different from 'sex'? How?

What's the difference between feminist archaeology and the archaeology of gender?

How might the Man the Hunter story influence modern gender roles?

What's your response to the critique that feminist archaeologists simply project liberal Western ideas about gender equity into an unknowable past?

Why did most archaeologists ignore gender for so long since it's such a basic way of organizing society?

What evidence is there that the practice of archaeology was/is androcentric?

What do you think of Janet Spector's narrative? Is it convincing? Is she guilty of stretching the evidence to make her point? (What is her point?)

What is the 'add women and stir' recipe for archaeological interpretation? How is Spector's work different from/an improvement on that model?

Things to Read

Battle-Baptiste, Whitney,
2011 *Black Feminist Archaeology*. Left Coast Press, Inc., Walnut Creek, California.

Conkey, Margaret and Joan Gero (Eds.)
1991 *Engendering Archaeology: Women and Prehistory*. Basil Blackwell, Cambridge, Massachusetts.

Dahlberg, Frances (ed.)
1983 *Woman the Gatherer*. Yale University Press, New Haven, Connecticut.

Deetz, James F.
1977 *In Small Things Forgotten: An Archaeology of Early American Life*. Anchor Books, New York.

Gero, Joan
1985 Socio-politics of Archaeology and the Woman-at-Home Ideology. *American Antiquity 50*:342–350.

Greer, Germaine
2008 *The Female Eunuch*. Harper Modern Classics, New York.

hooks, bell
1999 *Ain't I a Woman? Black Women and Feminism*. South End Press, Cambridge, Massachusetts.

Millet, Kate
2000 *Sexual Politics*. University of Illinois Press, Chicago.

Montagu, Ashley
1953 *The Natural Superiority of Women*. MacMillan, New York.

Paglia, Camille
1992 *Sex, Art, and American Culture: Essays*. Vintage Books, New York.

Seifert, Donna (Ed.)

1991 Gender in Historical Archaeology. *Historical Archaeology* *25*(4).

Shelly, Mary Wollstonecraft

2003 *Frankenstein or the Modern Prometheus*. Penguin Books, London.

Spector, Janet

1993 *What This Awl Means: Feminist Archaeology at a Wahpeteton Dakota Village*. Minnesota Historical Society Press, St. Paul.

Steinem, Gloria

1970 Women's Liberation Aims to Free Men, Too. *Washington Post* June 7, 1970.

Voss, Barbara and Robert Schmidt (Eds.)

2000 *Archaeologies of Sexuality*. Routledge, London.

Wollstonecraft, Mary

1996 *A Vindication of the Rights of Women*. Penguin Books, London.

CHAPTER 7
QUEER THEORY

*Queer is by definition at odds with the normal,
the legitimate, the dominant.*

David Halperin

What is Queer Theory?

Queer Theory (QT) is a series of ideas that **problematizes** what it means to be normal.

If that doesn't help, consider the fact that QT isn't really a theory at all in the sense of Darwin's thoughts about natural selection or the astronomers' Big Bang. These are ideas that explain the world, but QT is more of a way of looking at it from a different orientation and then taking action. In its activism, QT is a form of **critical theory** (see Chapter 4).

And now that we've got that out of the way, it's worth saying that QT isn't just a trendy way of referring to gay/lesbian or gender studies—although it does have a lot to say on the topic. In fact, although **LBGTQ** people started it, QT isn't their intellectual property at all. Anyone who feels that his or her

Archaeological Theory in a Nutshell: Adrian Praetzellis, 85–94.

intellectual position has been marginalized as unacceptable or unthinkable can apply it. To take up this oppositional position in relation to some idea or discourse is spoken of as *queering* it.

While feminists of the 1970s and '80s were pointing out the problems with Western society's androcentric biases, sexual minorities insisted that they were marginalized by the assumption of **heteronormalcy** on the part of pretty much everyone—including the feminists (see Chapter 6). The heteronormal view is the tacit expectation that heterosexuality is normal and natural, and that anything else is deviance.

Practitioners of QT will take on just about any **essentializing** doctrine. But their foundational problem is with the ideas that (1) human beings have basic natures that relate to their roles in reproduction and (2) social roles and sexual orientation flow 'naturally' from their biological sex. These ideas align one's biological sex with one's social role and sexual orientation. It is one of those notions that are powerful because we take them for granted and see no reason to problematize them. The effects of heteronormalcy extend into all aspects of life—consider the image that comes to mind when you think of the word 'family' and then think of the implications of being a non-heteronormal one in countries where it's illegal.

Although he didn't start it all, **Michel Foucault** was an intellectual father of the movement. (Hmmm. Perhaps I should *queer* that metaphor...) He pointed out that a society's attempts to control non-normative behavior begin by defining it as deviant and weird. Experts revered by Western nineteenth-century society (psychologists, criminalists, and so forth) created categories of people (such as the insane and the homosexual) whom they placed outside the range of 'normal.' Before this time, said Foucault, sodomy was a common sexual behavior, albeit an illegal one in many Western societies. After the experts did their studies, wrote them up in professional jargon, and published them in academic journals, the performers of the act were transformed into a deviant class of persons. Instead of being merely people whose sexual desire was out of sync with middle class values, they came to be thought of by society as sick and in need of help.

Early anthropologists had a hand in this, providing scientific validity to the idea that 'civilized' people (the White European middle class) were more morally evolved than 'savages.' Monogamy, for example, was considered the natural human condition. Obsessed as they were with the sexual side of relationships, Victorians classed polyandry and polygamy as unnatural and deviant. This is in spite of the fact that these practices were far more common worldwide than monogamy—more 'normal' one might say.

QT seeks to de-naturalize rigid sexual identities and to destabilize the whole concept of 'normal.'

Queer theory and archaeology

As we will soon cover some of the ground of **transgressive** archaeologies elsewhere in my little book (in Chapter 10), this section is going to emphasize the contribution of QT to the archaeology of non-heteronormal sexualities. It goes without saying that archaeologists never, or at least hardly ever, excavate direct evidence of sexual behavior. One exception is a group of seventeenth-century condoms excavated at Dudley Castle in England, but that's another story.

Archaeologists can be said to queer our own field when they go against any normative practice. As a discipline that's grounded in normative science, that can include taking seriously things that the mainstream either ignores as self-evident or avoids as overly transgressive. By this I mean a practice that passes the bounds of acceptable eccentricity and ventures into the realm of the weird and career damaging. The formal excavation of the contents of a 1991 Ford van by Adrian Myers and colleagues as a legitimate archaeological enterprise rather than as a piece of performance art is one of these queering projects. Its publication in various mainstream journals only goes to show how hard it is to shock the archaeological community.

I'll say again that QT isn't only about sexuality. And yet the strongest theme in queer archaeology has been to unsettle our

Egyptians Niankhkhnum and Khnumhotep shared a tomb and evidently considered themselves to be part of the same family. This and other wall decorations show their mutual affection.

assumptions about heterosexuality. Discussions about the relationships between the people whose buildings or tombs we dig up can no longer assume the 'normal.' Egyptology may be one of the most conservative segments of archaeological practice, and yet it has provided one of the premier examples of re-reading an artifact to see other possibilities. A case in point is Greg Reeder's study of the 5th dynasty depictions of Niankhkhnum and Khnumhotep in their joint tomb. These 4,300 year old paintings show the two men in various poses suggesting their strong affection: holding hands, face to face with touching noses, even kissing. A heteronormal interpretation might be that they were brothers. And perhaps they were. Both were married and had children. But, suggests Greg Reeder, the fact that they

88

are depicted in this way by a tradition that commonly showed conjugal relationships between husband and wife indicates that their families included each other regardless of whether their relationship had a sexual dimension or not.

QT analysis began and is most often practiced by deconstructing texts. The field of literary criticism has developed a whole set of established methods and jargon for doing its work. Although artifacts have been compared to and deconstructed like texts, the analogy breaks down past a point. In short, there is no widely accepted method of applying QT to archaeological sites and objects.

An example of queer archaeology[1]

Prisons are designed to be what sociologist Erving Goffman called "total institutions": isolated, self-contained physical environments with an imposed social structure. They are calculated to control inmates' physical movement and interactions. At least, that's the goal. One of the greatest benefits of text-added archaeology is its ability to get below the surface of institutions and uncover, quite literally, the lives of the people who experienced them. Archaeologists use the term *lived reality* to emphasize their aim of reconstructing ways of life in a manner that evokes empathy. The fact that seventeen large four-hole buttons were found in Area B wasn't of much general interest until El Casella figured out that they ended up there by means of actual human intention.

The Ross Female Factory was a women's prison. It operated from 1848 to 1854 in Tasmania, an island off the south coast of Australia, then a British colony. Most inmates had been convicted of what we would now call petty theft. They had stolen some inexpensive item from their employer. The Factory system was intended to reform women by means of Christian prayer and reflection, as well as providing useful training in the conventional female occupations of sewing, laundering, and cooking.

---

1 Eleanor Conlin Cassella, *Doing Trade* (2000).

Problem prisoners ended up on short rations in a four by six foot solitary cell. After a woman had served her prison term and been rehabilitated to the satisfaction of her jailers, she would be probationed out as a domestic servant to one of the island's colonists.

As inmates, the women lived in the part of the prison according to their status as either Crime Class (serving in the general population), in Solitary Cells, or Hiring Class (on probation as servants). Archaeologist Casella excavated a portion of each of these areas. Among the artifacts she found were buttons. Now these are very common on historic-era sites and by itself the discovery wouldn't put anyone in line for an Award of Merit. But archaeology is all about context. While the Hiring Class site had problems and Casella decided not to use it, the collections from under the Crime Class Dormitory and Solitary Cell floors had the kind of stratigraphic integrity and consistent dates that fit with the historic uses of these locations. In short, it was reasonable for her to assume that the objects represent activities that went on at these places during the prison era.

The first thing Casella noticed was that three times as many buttons were found in the Solitary Cells than in the Crime Class Dormitory. There was also a wider range of types (material, dimensions, and so on), many didn't come from prison issue clothing, and some had been intentionally modified. Considering how strictly the two locations were segregated, she reasoned that this non-uniform distribution must represent something other than just accidental loss.

But why would prisoners intentionally hoard *buttons* of all things? It seemed that these items had a value and a purpose that didn't relate to their usual function. The use of buttons as gambling tokens is well documented; and yet the Solitary Cells had no opportunity for gambling. But if they *were* tokens—essentially currency—they could have been the medium for trade. This led Casella to ask, "What forms of 'trade' may have fuelled this black market economy?" The answer is a mix of contraband and sexual favors.

Did inmates of a women's prison use buttons as a form of illicit currency even when in solitary confinement? This trade may have paid for sexual favors and luxury items.

Court documents show that black market liquor, tea, and so forth could be obtained in Solitary, presumably through a medium of trade. Opportunistic sexual encounters were also a fact of life in female prisons. The 'English vice,' as it was called, was sometimes fueled by smuggled-in luxuries and other enticements, and sometimes by strong emotional attachments. Whether carried on for reasons of sustained love, casual sex, or both, these relationships were part of the prison's social structure. In a nearby female factory, the ill treatment of a woman in Solitary led to an all-out revolt orchestrated by her lover.

The presence of apparent trade tokens in Solitary is emblematic of the prison's underground culture. Solitary was designed as the most cut off part of this isolated institution, where inmates would be entirely stripped of their independence. Instead, it appears to have been the center of the underground economy, for it was in Solitary that these small luxuries were most needed. It looks like the very scene of punishment turned into the center of resistance.

El Casella's example is effective partly because of the contrast between the institution's architecture and social purpose, and because of the lives inmates made for themselves. The first was rigid, uniform, moralistic, and controlled. Yet below the surface was an entire underground culture of complex emotional and economic relationships, fueled in part by sex and contraband.

The sum up

Many people are unhappy about the potential of QT to supplant feminist and LGBTQ studies. Although they share some general goals, by definition QT is not exclusively focused on these issues. Some fear that the adoption of QT will water down feminist and LGBTQ politics. And then there's the identity issue. If queering is not a LGBTQ thing, can a married, heterosexual declare him or herself 'queer'? One can foresee a situation in which sexual minorities become minorities in their own academic fields.

In archaeology, this translates into the concern that QT is merely a contrarian stance. As it does not focus on any particular research theme or question, might QT lead to studies whose only commonality is their self-declared queer-ness?

Although it's risky to generalize, it seems to me that many archaeologists still associate QT with digging up homosexuals and, consequently, that it hasn't much to do with their particular work. One of the functions of applying any theory or approach in archaeology is to stimulate the archaeological imagination. We can call it queering or something else. It doesn't really matter. QT helps the archaeologist expand what is possible, to put new meanings onto familiar objects, to 'think the unthinkable.'

Questions to Discuss

Is the queer critique of heteronormalcy valid considering that sexual and gender minorities are just that—minorities?

Are members of a group (ethnic, gender, religious, and so on) better qualified than non-members to study it? What do cultural insiders bring to research that outsiders lack? And what do outsiders bring?

What are the ethics of an outsider presenting an interpretation to which insiders object? Where does self-preservation end and censorship begin?

What do you think about Foucault's idea that the creation of 'experts' leads to the rationalization of culture-bound, taken-for-granted ideas? How does this analysis relate to the practice of archaeology?

To what extent do archaeological experts (like me, for example) draw the boundaries of legitimate research and what is acceptably transgressive?

What other areas of archaeology and contemporary culture in general (universities, for example) might benefit from queering? What unthinkable topics should be discussed?

Things to Read

Cassella, Eleanor Conlin

2000 'Doing Trade': A Sexual Economy of Nineteenth-Century Australian Female Convict Prisons. *World Archaeology* 32(2):209–221.

Foucault, Michel

1978 *The History of Sexuality.* Translated by Robert Hurley. Pantheon Books, New York.

1995 *Discipline and Punish: The Birth of the Prison.* Translated by Alan Sheridan. Vintage Books, New York.

Goffman, Erving

1961 *Asylums.* Anchor Books, New York.

Halperin, David

1996 *Saint Foucault: Towards a Gay Hagiography.* Oxford University Press, Oxford, UK.

Myers, Adrian, Greg Bailey, Cassie Newland, John Schofield, Anna Nilsson, and Steve Davis

2008 Excavating a 1991 Ford Van. *SAA Archaeological Record* 8(4):34–40.

Reeder, Greg

2005 Same-Sex Desire, Conjugal Constructs, and the Tomb of Niankhkhnum and Khnumhotep. *World Archaeology* 32(2):193–208.

CHAPTER 8

STRUCTURALISM

[Animal totems] are chosen not because they are good to eat but because they are good to think.

Claude Lévi-Strauss

What is structuralism?

Structuralism is a theory that sees every aspect of culture as the creation of unconsciously applied rules, like those of language, based in the unchanging structure of the human mind. According to the structuralists, the mind doesn't begin as an empty page ready to be printed on by experience. Instead, it filters information and organizes the data according to certain pre-existing structures in order to make sense of it all. These structures, they say, underlie how we perceive reality, create culture, and ultimately condition how we make history.

Although linguist **Ferdinand de Saussure** didn't start it all, he gets a lot of the credit (or blame). De Saussure drew a useful distinction between language and speech, which, being Swiss,

Archaeological Theory in a Nutshell: Adrian Praetzellis, 95–107.

he called *langue* and *parole*. The first is the system of rules (grammar, syntax) that we use to construct a sentence. The second is the speech acts created when people apply the rules when having a conversation. The rules are there in the background, and no one thinks about them when they're talking. The signs (words) are arbitrary symbols for things—cat, *chat*, and *gato* all refer to the same species of beast in three languages. Therefore, say the structuralists, every human population generates different symbols to express the reality of their culture and history but always according to the same underlying *structure*.

The form and arrangement of material culture (including archaeological artifacts) are, so they say, structured by syntax-like rules that can be deduced. And when you understand the structure, you can crack the code of any population's particular cultural symbols.

Anthropologist **Claude Lévi-Strauss** used structural analysis to understand *totemism*—the way some societies divide themselves into groups that claim a particular supernatural animal, their totem, as their ancestor. Why, asked the wise, did these people identify with those particular beasts? It might be understandable, they mused, if members of the turtle clan are particularly slow or the eagle clan is known for its skill in the hunt. But, according to Claude, this was the wrong way to look at it. He believed that the relationship between the creatures and the clans they represent is based on characteristics that the scientific mind could not deduce because it is has no apparent purpose: the turtle lives low, the eagle lives high; the turtle is hard, the eagle is soft. The rule requires that clan totems have opposite characteristics and has nothing to do with the supposed nobility of the eagle or the strength of the bear.

Now, Lévi-Strauss would say that this rule is generated by the structure of the mind and shows that it processes reality as a series of binary oppositions: low/high, hard/soft, male/female, sky/earth, and so forth. If you accept what he has to say, structural analysis is a very powerful tool for understanding why people do what they do.

Back (temporarily) to Karl Marx. His vision was in some ways structuralist, for, said he, (1) human societies are molded by a hidden structure; (2) this structure is an eternal fact of reality; and (3) it is the root cause and generator of cultures in all their variability. Marxist analysis envisions a clear hierarchy: the material conditions of life determine social structure that creates ideologies like religion. A structuralist like Lévi-Strauss, on the other hand, begins with the structure of the mind. Uncle Karl also believed that there is an underlying structure that creates the human world. But for him it is economics and has nothing whatsoever to do with the mind. Lévi-Strauss's analysis would have left Marx cold, and I suspect he would have shrugged it off as a bourgeois ideology that serves to mask reality.

Both Lévi-Strauss and Marx were convinced that an immutable structure shapes human history and cultures; they just disagreed on what it looks like. So be sure to say what you mean if you call someone a structuralist.

Structuralism and archaeology

As the same grammar underlays everything produced by a culture, the beauty of the structuralist method is that it identifies a harmony between functionally dissimilar objects and forms. By identifying the rules by which elements are put together, the archaeologist creates (or identifies) conformity between things that are entirely dissimilar on the surface. The same rules govern the layout of a house and the pattern of refuse disposal, the decorations on pots, and burial practices.

You don't need contextual information to do structuralism since it's based on timeless principles. So, as they have no written or oral sources to help interpret their sites, prehistorians took to structuralism early. Parietal art (pictographs and petroglyphs) are mysterious and awe-inspiring links to the minds of early humans. But what did they mean to the people who made them? Archaeologists like **André Leroi-Gourhan** saw structural analysis as a great alternative to the functionalists who saw

Structuralists like André Leroi-Gourhan didn't really care what Paleolithic cave art depicted. Rather, they wanted to know what it represented to the people who created it. The auroch and horse (*left and right*) were the symbols of femaleness and maleness, respectively, according to André.

these drawings of animals and symbols as art for art's sake and, later, as magical artifacts drawn to help control the forces of nature by symbolically 'killing' prey. Instead of focusing on the signs as symbols in a Paleolithic cave, Leroi-Gourhan looked at the arrangement of the elements to each other, identifying some elements (and some portions of the cave) as having male and others as having female associations.

Structuralist archaeologists were criticized for their uncon-cern with the historical context of the artifacts they interpret. This is hardly surprising. If you think that binary oppositions like raw/cooked and public/private are universal, then it's not at all important to work out the meaning of the symbols them-selves. This is convenient, as prehistorians have only analogy to help them understand what artifacts meant to their creators. Historical archaeologists never had that problem. Because the people they study wrote things down, they can avoid the pre-historians' problem of overgeneralized analogy by combining it with the direct historical approach (see Chapter 1).

In his nifty structural analysis of houses in the fortress of Masada, David Small used the writings of contemporary historians as well as the Mishnah, a compendium of Jewish rules of conduct and custom. These independent sources (both primary and secondary) helped determine the historic and cultural context in which the buildings were created. Small showed among other things how the design of buildings emerged from the religious regulation of male/female contact. I was convinced by his argument and felt I'd got an important insight into the how these peoples' ideologies unconsciously structured their world.

Accepting the structuralist premise that the human mind is indeed structured in this way and that these binaries are the same across time and culture are big steps that many archaeologists aren't willing to take. It is a **normative** view of culture that assumes all the members of a group apply the same meanings to things. One might ask if everyone who lived at Masada followed the rules exactly as they were set down in the Mishnah? And feminist archaeology would certainly have a problem with a supposedly universal male/female binary structure that is based on cultural notions of gender (see Chapter 6). But more of that later.

An example of structuralist archaeology[1]

Jim Deetz stood puzzling over three piles of ceramics. Each was from a different archaeological site in New England, the northeast corner of what is now the United States. The earliest dated to the early seventeenth century, the middle from about 1660 to 1760, and the last was from the late eighteenth century. Deetz noticed that they were very different in quantity, color, and vessel forms. Why was this? Most archaeologists might have said the pots reflected changes in fashion, in technology, and trade. But Deetz was never conventional and wasn't satisfied with this kind of explanation. Instead, he saw in these

---

1 James F. Deetz, *In Small Things Forgotten* (1996).

changes clues to a profound alteration in how people thought, lived, and saw their world.

What do ceramic pots, gravestones, and houses have in common? They are all items of material culture, "that section of our physical environment that we modify through culturally determined behavior," according to Deetz. By studying what people created according to their unconscious mental templates, we can, Deetz felt, discover things about their culture at a deep level, things they didn't know themselves. This archaeology wasn't to be only about the things people possessed but how they thought.

We do history to understand ways of life, not just to document important events. From the establishment of English colonies in North America in the early 1600s to the late eighteenth century, the culture of the colonists and their descendants changed profoundly. Until about 1660 the colonists' way of life and thought was quite English, according to Deetz. They lived under English law, and even that most American of celebrations, Thanksgiving, was a variation on the English harvest festival. They tended to live in villages much like those of the old country.

But after the mid-seventeenth century there was a drift away from this 'parent culture,' and for perhaps a century a folk tradition developed. This was something distinct and different. Puritan religion declined and the old corporate values began to give way to an emphasis on individualism. The late 1800s saw what Deetz calls a "re-Anglicization" of colonial culture in which this folk culture was transformed by more intense contact with the rationalist values of Europe. By the end of the eighteenth century the old corporate values had largely disappeared. The individual had become, as now, the most important unit in American society.

How did the change from English culture to colonial folk to re-Anglicized culture occur? How could people's worldview be so transformed that individualization came to be seen as desirable and right? And how did material culture help in this process, not just reflecting the changes but actually enabling them? These were the questions in Deetz's mind. But first, I'll describe some of the changes he observed in foodways, grave-stones, and houses.

The colonists who came to North America in the early 1600s brought the customs of old England. Their meals of meat were stews cooked and served from a communal pot. This and other messes were eaten from a wooden trencher, a sort of all-purpose tray often shared by two people at the same meal. Ceramic bowls and plates were relatively rare and were most likely used for display. As time passed, the use of plates and specialized serving vessels increased. By the late eighteenth century archaeologists find that sets of dishes—each with its own specialized function—were common. Food consumption had changed from a communal activity to an individuated one. Similarly, as Deetz pointed out, the idea of one person per plate is symmetrical and balanced, while sharing is not.

A gravestone has advantages over other artifacts: it bears the date it was made (or close enough) and generally stays where it's put. Gravestones also reflect a culture's attitude toward death and its philosophy of life. Borrowing from his work with Ed Dethlefsen, Deetz documented changes in gravestone design from the mid-1600s to the early nineteenth century. Early stones depict naturalistic winged skulls and convey the idea that death and decay is our common fate. As time passed, the image of the skull became increasingly abstract until it was almost unrec-ognizable, and the cherub, a popular English design, came to dominate by the mid-1700s—Deetz's period of re-Anglicization. The message of death and decay was being replaced by the more uplifting notion of resurrection. Then, by the 1790s a third image, a willow tree and urn, supplanted the chubby-cheeked cherub. In less than 200 years gravestones had changed from a reminder of the decay that awaits us all to commemorations of the individual and his or her status in life.

Houses are Deetz's third artifact category. Initially, English colonists built what they knew and had no need for architects. Their houses were of traditional design, built by craftsmen from a cultural template of what constituted a proper dwelling. The

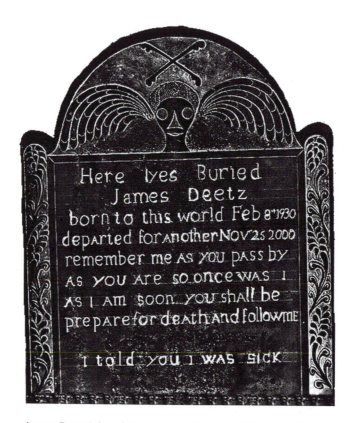

Here lyes Buried
James Deetz
born to this world Feb 8ᵗʰ 1930
departed for another NOV 25 2000
remember me AS YOU PASS by
AS YOU ARE SO ONCE WAS I
AS I AM SOON YOU shALL be
prepare for death and follow me.

I told YOU I WAS SICK

James Deetz's headstone, carved by Dave Wheelock, is now installed in St. Peter's Cemetery, Westernport, Maryland. It incorporates one of Jim's favorite seventeenth century motifs, the stylized winged skull, as well as a typical epitaph of the era (the poem, I mean, not the parting joke!).

visitor would step directly from the outside into the living quarters. There were few specialized spaces and privacy was inconceivable in the communal sleeping room that often housed both servants and master. As its residents' needs changed, so did their house, sprouting rooms and additions somewhat organically. With the mid-1700s came designs that seemed to fit the new way of thinking and more rigid social relationships. Inside, the old corporate, undifferentiated spaces were gone, now divided into specialized rooms where one's privacy could be assured by doors and hallways. Outside, where the traditional house was asymmetrical and organic the Georgian house was balanced, showing control over the forces of nature within and without, and the orderliness of the lives it sheltered.

We can see a variety of binary structures in the changes exhibited by these artifacts: communal/individual, public/private, natural substance/artificial substance, emotion/intellect, asymmetrical/symmetrical. These are not just word games to the structuralist. They are the actual categories the brain uses to process information. In the 200 years covered by Deetz's study, increased social distance between people made these transformed artifacts and practices acceptable as they accommodated and enhanced the new culture. Lévi-Strauss might have said they became "good to think."

Easy to read, *In Small Things Forgotten* is a brilliant synthesis that is still one of the best examples of structuralist archaeology decades after it was published. What other archaeologist was using images, plans, art, design, and even sound as data? Astonishingly, it was written in a single draft over about six weeks. We can't talk about Deetz's structuralism without mentioning Henry Glassie, one of the most amazing scholars of his generation. Deetz had been developing his ideas for several years (I still have the class notes), but it was through his friendship and exchange of ideas with Glassie that he came to realize the power of the structuralist method. Don't be put off by the title of Glassie's book, *Folk Housing in Middle Virginia*. Read it, then read it again.

The sum up

So if structuralism is such a powerful tool, why aren't more archaeologists using it? If I were a structuralist, I might suggest that it reflects the binary division between American empiricism and European theorizing. To use a structural metaphor, **hermeneutic** understandings are 'soft' and ambiguous, while science is 'hard' and produces results that can be tested with recognized metrics.

I'm not the first to suggest that, but it's only partly correct. Ultimately, the structuralist approach in archaeology has been supplanted by (wait for it...) **poststructuralism**. This term is used to describe an orientation away from explanations such as Marxism and structuralism and towards contextual interpretations: the idea that the meaning(s) of material culture is variable and can only be derived from an understanding of the context in which it was created. Most of the approaches described in the rest of this book can be considered poststructuralist.

Leroi-Gourhan, for example, took all the elements in his cave as one data set, although they may have been created over as long as 25,000 years. Did the symbols mean the same to their creators across this huge swath of time? Many postprocessual archaeologists have come to see structuralism as a method that places itself outside deconstruction. That is, it requires symbols (open/closed, public/private, and so on) to have the same meanings across time and regardless of context.

Unlike David Small at Masada, Deetz's method wasn't conventionally scientific. It was inductive, like much of his work. Deetz would start with patterns in the material record, look for a method through which to make sense of them, and see how these changes were concomitant with ideological changes in larger society. The freedom to be inductive continues to attract archaeologists who feel restricted by the scientific method, want to engage the emotions as well as the intellect, and to move in areas of interpretation where statistical probability is not the ultimate test of worth.

On the other hand, many archaeologists have come to view the structuralist method as just another form of essentialism whose tidy explanations are satisfying to the audience because they are based on familiar tropes. Maybe… but it seems to me that structuralism doesn't necessarily claim to offer testable explanations, just possibilities that stand or fall on their plausibility.

Questions to Discuss

What does the word 'structure' mean to a Levi-Straussian structuralist? Why are both Deetz and Marx considered structuralists? What
do they have in common?

How do archaeologists use analogy in their interpretations? How
does structuralism relate to archaeologists' use of analogy and the
direct historical approach?

Might the structuralists' categories (Deetz's for example) be nothing more than modern impositions on minds that were nothing like
ours? How would you know one way or the other?

Does structuralism have any room for individual agency? After all,
isn't everyone a unique individual, his or her own beliefs and understandings deriving from his or her culture, life experience, habitus,
and so forth?

Things to Read

de Saussure, Ferdinand
1986 *Course in General Linguistics.* Translated by Roy Harris. Open Court, Chicago.

Deetz, James F.
1996 *In Small Things Forgotten: An Archaeology of Early American Life.* Anchor Books, New York.

Dethlefsen, Edwin and James Deetz
1966 Death's Heads, Cherubs, and Willow Trees: Experimental Archaeology in Colonial Cemeteries. *American Antiquity* 31(4):502–510.

Glassie, Henry
1976 *Folk Housing in Middle Virginia.* University of Tennessee Press, Knoxville.

Leroi-Gourhan, André
1957 *Prehistoric Man.* Kensington, New York.

Levi-Strauss, Claude
1963 *Structural Anthropology.* Basic Books, New York.
1971 *Totemism.* Beacon Press, Boston.

Small, David B.
1987 Toward a Competent Structuralist Archaeology: A Contribution from Historical Studies. *Journal of Anthropological Archaeology* 6:105–121.

CHAPTER 9

AGENCY, STRUCTURE, AND STRUCTURATION

Institutions do not just work 'behind the backs' of the social actors who produce and reproduce them.

Anthony Giddens

What is agency?

Agency is the idea that individuals are the active creators of their own lives, rather than the hostages of forces they can't influence. If that seems rather self-evident and hardly worthy of its own body of theory, you probably skipped the chapters on Marxism, Critical Theory, and Structuralism (see Chapters 3, 4, and 8).

I'll re-cap. It has been suggested that **structuralism** views the relation between individuals and society as rather mechanical, in a determinist way some might say. Society, it's claimed, develops structures, such as classes that people like you and me accept more or less passively as 'natural' until and unless some revolutionary movement breaks the cycle of social reproduction.

Archaeological Theory in a Nutshell: Adrian Praetzellis, 109–118.

But is that true? Can individuals (agents) actually have an effect on society? Dissatisfied with the emphasis on the power of structure over individuals, British sociologist Anthony Giddens came up with the idea of **structuration** that looks at the relationship more subtly and from the opposite direction. Giddens doesn't say that these social structures don't exist or aren't important; he's a sociologist after all. His idea is that individuals understand these structures and actively work the system to their own benefit. In other words, they are agents in the creation of their own lives.

Giddens makes fun of **Louis Althusser**, yet another famously dead French social theorist (see Chapter 4) who, according to the Brit, assumes that people are completely taken in by the dominant ideology. According to Giddens, if what Althusser

Anthony Giddens (that's Lord Giddens of Southgate to you) came up with the idea of structuration. In modern politics, it has been used to support the so-called "third way"—a fusion of conservative economics with liberal social policies.

says were true, these people would be "cultural dopes of an astonishing mediocrity." Ouch. Take that, Louis!

Agency is the mechanism by which structuration operates in daily life. Agency links the idea of structuration with the actions of real people (their agency) and gives us a way to understand these acts. **Practice theory** seeks to work between structure and agency, egged on by *doxa* (ideas that are so set in our minds that they 'go without saying'). And this is where archaeology comes in. For if archaeologists (particularly historical archaeologists) do one thing well, it's teasing out the details of individual lives.

Agency and archaeology

Archaeologists love to raid other disciplines for their ideas. And why not? It's a reciprocal relationship. As the insights of one set of ideas become entrenched in archaeology, there are always going to be people who will point out how this particular depiction of the world is inadequate.

The idea of agency took off among archaeologists partly in response to (wait for it...) the New Archeology. You may recall from Chapter 1 that practitioners of the latter liked to think of societies as whole systems whose individual cultural components functioned rather like an organism to maintain and reproduce itself. While everything worked together, the culture flourished. But when the feedback loop malfunctioned and the culture didn't adapt to new circumstances, problems emerged. Now, this is a satisfying and coherent vision of how the world works... but it is rather soulless. What's missing, said some archaeologists, is how individuals' own beliefs about their situation—their individual goals, intentions, and most importantly, their actions—affected the system.

Now actions, of course, create material culture. And understanding that stuff is what archaeology is all about.

If Giddens is right and people act with intention and understanding of their social situation, then they will resist structures that oppose their interests. For example, if a factory worker feels like he is being underpaid, he may resist by calling in sick, working slowly, or even sabotaging the equipment. People can use artifacts to symbolize and reinforce their resistance. In some situations they create their social identity around these symbols.

Jim Symonds, for example, showed how Scottish highlanders' querns (rock slabs used to grind wheat) came to represent resistance to laws originating down south in London that made them use only government-sanctioned flourmills. These rural Scots said no thanks—though perhaps not so politely—and each household kept using its own quern until English soldiers confiscated them and dumped them in a lake. In short, the crofters resisted the incursion of English ideas in the only way they could, using the most ancient of traditional artifacts.

Archaeologists mostly dig up the results of small-scale decisions and events. As resistance often occurs at this scale, we're in a good position to be able to see individual agency in the past. Resistance at this scale often went unrecorded by the people who practiced it because

- ◎ it was illegal, or at least frowned upon, or
- ◎ nobody at the time thought it was worth writing down, or
- ◎ being poor and powerless, the people didn't think they had anything important to say.

Archaeology is often the only way to reconstruct the experience of **subaltern** groups whom we might otherwise think of as merely the victims of history rather than its creators.

An example of structure and agency in archaeology 1

Strictly by the numbers, South Carolina in the early and mid-eighteenth century was more African than European. But although the white slave owner class called the tune, the sheer size of the black population gave members of this group some autonomy over the details of their daily existence. What did these people think of their condition? For one thing, they

---

1 Leland Ferguson, *Struggling with Pots in Colonial South Carolina* (1991).

actively resisted the system that plucked them from their West African villages by trying to escape. But Ferguson suggests that they also developed more subtle and essentially unconscious responses.

The white plantation owners competed among themselves for political domination using a complex set of symbols such as Georgian houses, formal gardens, and other artifacts designed (according to critical theorists, see Chapter 4) to convince others of their natural superiority. All very impressive, but did their slaves buy this hegemonic ideology? Did it become part of their way of looking at the world? Ferguson thinks not. His evidence comes from the foodways of the era.

Consider the dining practices of the plantation owning class. Their meals were served in individual vessels whose high cost was reflected in their fancy ceramic fabric and decoration. Fastidious diners were careful to replace their outmoded styles with the Next Big Thing. One dare not lag too far behind the wave of fashion lest people might think you can't afford new stuff or (horrors!) that you're out of touch. Any similarity between this pattern and archaeologists' appetite for the theoretical Next Big Thing is purely coincidental.

While the residents of the big house fretted over the relative merits of English creamware and Chinese porcelain, their slaves lived a very different reality. Most were either West African by birth or only one or two generations from their ancestral homeland. Their culture, including foodways, was largely African. While most of the gourds and basketry items they used to store and prepare food decayed long ago, their Colono ware ceramics have survived. *Colono* is a type of handmade, low-fired earthenware made by people of West African descent until the mid-nineteenth century. It makes up about 70 percent of pots found in South Carolina slave quarters. Jars and bowls are the most common Colono ware forms found in the state. The jars have a globular shape with a round handle and a wide flaring rim; they come in two sizes that hold about

1.75 and 5 liters (about 4 pints and 1-1/3 gallons, respectively). Colono ware bowls are wide and shallow, and hold about 1 liter (about 1/2 gallon).

How did people use these items? Most jar fragments found by archaeologists have burned surfaces, showing where they have been scorched in a cooking fire. Earthenware vessels are preferred by many present day Africans as well as Southern cooks of all ethnicities, since they cook slower than metal pots. In West Africa, a common meal consists of starch—rice or millet—a sauce, and a small amount of fish or meat. The starch is cooked in large jars; the sauce is made in smaller ones. When it's all nicely cooked, the starch is dished up onto a bowl with a gourd dipper. The diner picks up a ball of starch, dips it in the sauce, and pops it into his or her mouth. Less than 2 percent of Colono ware bowls from South Carolina have wear marks that show their owners used some kind of implement to eat from it. Interviews conducted in the 1930s indicate that a century earlier some enslaved people ate in the West African tradition, using their fingers rather than the forks and spoons of their white masters.

In contrast to the fashion-dependent and status-enhancing ceramics prized by the plantation owners, Colono ware was a folk product. Its design and production were passed almost unchanged down through the generations. Examples of individual forms vary little in shape, and almost none shows any decoration. From this, Ferguson concludes that these slaves were not copying the hierarchical way of the white masters. While the latter used pots as weapons in the battle to affirm and improve their social status, to African and African-American slaves their undecorated pots represented traditional social ties and group identity.

Ferguson suggests that while whites may have believed that their ostentatious material culture awed their slaves into submission—making them internalize feelings of

Just one in a crowd. There's a lot of debate about the ability of the individual to affect change in society or even control his or her own. While structural models emphasize the power of forces outside our control, other approaches allow some agency… and some hope.

inferiority—there's no evidence that the strategy actually worked on a group level. On the contrary. The traditional Colono ceramics strengthened values of community and the bonds of tradition by helping people maintain long-established cultural practices. In this way, says Ferguson, enslaved people lived a kind of practical, unconscious resistance to whites' ideology by just doing their everyday activities in the old way. By just being themselves.

The sum up

Changing the scale of analysis humanizes the past and provides us some great insights. It gives us access to inspiring stories of cultural tenacity in the face of inhuman treatment and shows how people can indeed make a difference.

However, as Karl Marx wrote, "We are both the creators and creatures of history." Personalizing the past is not without risk. By emphasizing the efficacy of individual acts one may be left with an exaggerated idea of individuals' ability to make change. That can trivialize the coercive power of social structures, with the result that subalterns can be held responsible for their own disadvantaged condition: it's called blaming the victim. Social critics on the political left have pointed out that Anthony Giddens was close advisor to Tony Blair, prime minister of the UK from 1994 to 1997. Blair continued Margaret Thatcher's trends of privatizing public services, economic deregulation, and a general move toward making individuals (rather than government) responsible to fix society's problems.

So, yet again we are faced with the paradox that interpretive lenses invariably block out the light of some important aspects of social reality in order to reveal others that would otherwise be overpowered. The idea of agency is a sometimes-useful representation of a portion of reality. The map, however, is not the territory.

Questions to Discuss

What is the relationship between structure and agency? What does 'structuration' mean and how does it contribute to this discussion?

To what degree is the scholarly emphasis on agency just a reflection of Western culture's concern with individualism? Is agency a useful idea by which to examine societies that emphasize the group rather than the person? Or is there something universal about individual rights and aspirations? Is the emphasis on agency merely an optimistic way of interpreting past atrocities?

What were the limits of the enslaved South Carolinians' agency?

How can we identify individuals in the archaeological record?

If we emphasize individuals' roles, what's to prevent a return to the Great Man interpretation that sees change as the result of the important actions of exceptional individuals?

Things to Read

Dobres, Marcia-Anne and John Robb

2000 Agency in archaeology: paradigm or platitude? In Marcia-Anne Dobres and John Robb (Eds.), *Agency in Archaeology* (pp. 3–17). Routledge, London.

Ferguson, Leland

1991 Struggling with Pots in Colonial South Carolina. In Randall McGuire and Robert Paynter (Eds.), *The Archaeology of Inequality* (pp. 28–39). Blackwell, Oxford, UK.

Giddens, Anthony

1979 *Central Problems in Social Theory.* MacMillan, Basingstoke, UK.

Marx, Karl and Freidrich Engels

1967 *The Communist Manifesto.* Penguin Classics, London.

Pauketat, Timothy

2001 Practice and history in archaeology: An emerging paradigm. *Anthropological Theory* 1(1):73–98.

Symonds, James

2010 Poverty & Progress in the Age of Improvement: Evidence from the Isle of South Uist in the Outer Hebrides of Scotland. *Historical Archaeology* 45(3):106–120.

CHAPTER 10

TRANSGRESSIVE ARCHAEOLOGIES

*The birth of the reader must be at
the cost of the death of the Author.*

Roland Barthes

What are transgressive archaeologies?

Transgressive archaeologies are approaches to presenting the archaeological past that are outside the conventional scholarly mode. Yes, I made this category up, although it is related to queering archaeology and **Queer Theory**, which I dealt with way back in Chapter 7. What I call transgressive archaeologies came about when some archaeologists got dissatisfied with the usual way of doing things. Some people—not many, this is very much a minority enterprise—took to presenting their insights through poetry, fiction, theatre, and multimedia opera, in addition to the usual way.

This will take some explaining.

Archaeological Theory in a Nutshell: Adrian Praetzellis, 119–131.

Why is a mass-market novel like a realistic painting of a bowl of fruit? Both are easy to comprehend because we are familiar with the genres they represent. Unlike Andy Warhol's famous picture of a Campbell's soup can, there are no hidden meanings in the fruit painter's exercise in form, color, and perspective. The novel and the picture are both **univocal**. What the reader/viewer takes from the reading or viewing is just what the creator intended and no more. We are comfortable with the experience and derive a satisfaction, what **Roland Barthes** calls **"pleasure,"** from the predictability and the feeling of completeness we get from it. In Barthes's terms, uncomplicated novels and representational art are examples of **"readerly"** works—products created to be fully comprehensible to their audience.

On the other hand, says Barthes, there are **"writerly"** works. The atonal and quite non-whistleable music of Aaron Copeland. James Joyce's seemingly subjectless prose. The abstract sculpture of Alexander Calder. These don't offer easy understanding. In fact, much of their meaning comes from what the audience brings to the experience. The good conceptual artist is a skilled provoker of response. There is often no feeling of finality when the performance ends or the reader shuts the book. Just the reverse. The audience has struggled with the artist's intentional **multivocality**. You may feel drained by participating in the creation of the meaning of what you've just seen. Dealing with these works is unsettling. Worst of all, it provides no closure. What does the piece mean? You have to decide.

Barthes saw all cultural constructions from novels to sporting events as complex **texts** that could be "read." By the **"death of the author,"** he means that multivocality has abolished the division of labor between the producer (author) and the consumer (reader) of meaning.

Transgressive archaeologies and archaeology

At this point, the reader (if I can still use the word) may be asking her or himself what all this has to do with archaeology. Well here it is.

I started this section by saying that transgressive archaeologies emerged out of some archaeologists' frustration with the customary genres of scholarly expression: the site report, the conference paper, the journal article. In general, these modes are decidedly readerly. They are familiar and comfortable. Like the art-class painting of fruit in a bowl, they are univocal. And like the final chapter of a mystery novel that reveals all the red herrings and hidden motives, they appear 'finished.' But the intelligent reader recognizes this characteristic for what it is: a device, an artificial winding-up for the purpose of what Barthes would call *pleasure*. The meaning of an object or site is full of contingencies; it has no last word, no satisfying sum-up. Yet the convention of scholarly presentation insists on it.

Did I say they were frustrated? I might also have said fed up. The practice of archaeology has emotional and aesthetic qualities as well as intellectual ones, and the scientific ideal that encourages practitioners to segment their humanity has limits to its usefulness. Archaeologists' desire to do something writerly (although they might not use the term) stemmed from the fact that archaeological understanding is not the linear process into which the norms of scholarship force their interpretations. This left some people feeling constrained and wanting an outlet for their stifled creativity. Janet Spector hints at this in the introduction to her book, *What This Awl Means* (see Chapter 6).

Although the transgressive few use a variety of modes, they have some common goals: to engage the audience's emotions and senses, and to inject some playfulness into earnest academic settings. Many performances take place at venues set aside by custom for highly ritualized contests of intellectual acuity—academic conferences. This adds to the shock of the unexpected and, in the best tradition of multivocality, often creates that nervous unsettled feeling among attendees that Barthes calls "jouissance," the evil twin of his "pleasure."

It is a bit misleading of me to say that the 'goal' of writerly work in archaeology is to take the reader out of the mode of consumer and into the producer of meaning. For the work's

Which is 1850s lawyer and cultural go-between Josiah Gallup… and which is your humble author dressed up and playing him at an academic conference? The scenario asks what the subjects of archaeology would think of our interpretations of the things they left behind. Probably nothing good, we conclude. (Gallup's on the left, by the way.)

creator is, after all, still in the position of doing the writing for somebody else to read. Creating a writerly work may be as much about the archaeologist awakening his or her own creativity as it is about communicating the result to an audience. Sometimes more so.

Believing that the transgressive archaeologist is trying to conjure a specific past for others to admire, some critics get huffy. But the real purpose is to build a bridge: between a past that the archaeologist knows she can never experience and herself in the here and now. She uses the aesthetic tools that please her in a self-conscious act, and both artist and audience come away with what they will.

An example of transgressive archaeology[1]

Imagine you are at an archaeology conference. Half a dozen sessions are going on simultaneously, mostly structured around lectures organized by topic. A speaker stands up. He talks for 20 minutes. He sits down. And on to the next. Occasionally there's some discussion. Dress is usually casual and the political climate quite lefty, but it's a formal structure, and speakers are careful about what they say. There's a lot of furtive peeking at name badges to see if there's someone more important around to talk to.

Once in a while an effort is made to create new ways of presentation. Agendas are set, meetings convened, and everyone nods. The topic usually sinks without a trace.

Now imagine a conference symposium where participants are asked not to cite their sources and not to stick to demonstrable lines of evidence. Instead of saying only what they could support with fact, they are told to use their imagination to express what their archaeological sites *might* mean. To use any theatrical and literary device they fancy to engage the audience. And to use the word 'I' liberally. The result was three symposia at successive Society for Historical Archaeology annual conferences: *Archaeologists as Storytellers, Storytellers II: The Sequel,* and *Storytellers III: They're Baaack!* Writing about them is a very poor way to represent performances that had sounds and visual effects, costumes, and interactions with the audience, so you'll have to do what the participants did... and use your imagination.

In the first symposium, nine experienced archaeologists used a variety of modes to tell their stories: 'found' diaries, conversations, an oral history, historic accounts, and a play. Organized as a series of diary entries by the successive residents of a Massachusetts farm, Mary Beaudry's *Farm Journal*

---

1 Mary Praetzellis (editor), *Archaeologists as Storytellers* (1998).

CROWNE PLAZA
THEATRE

 Ladies Are Requested To Kindly Remove Their Hats.

ARCHAEOLOGISTS AS
STORYTELLERS II:
THE SEQUEL

BROUGHT TO THE STAGE BY MRS. MARY PRAETZELLIS

Thursday Jan 8, 1998

1:20 *Slaves, Rings, and Rubbish* (Mr. M. Hall)

1:40 *A Lost Memoir of a Lowell Boardinghouse Keeper*
(Ms. M. Beaudry)

2:00 *Fort Frederica's Hidden Past or*
Tales a Pot might Tell (Ms. A. Yentsch)

2:20 *"I Never Expect to Preach There Again."* ... (Ms. R. Ryder)

INTERMISSION (2:40-3:00)

3:00 *Red Light Voices* (Ms. J. Costello and Ms .J. Tordoff)

3:20 *Plantation Dialogs: A Conversation in One Act and*
Two Centuries (Mr. D. Mouer and Ms. Y. Edwards-Ingram)

3:40 *The Tale of Fermin Valenzuela*...(Mr. A. and Ms. M. Praetzellis)

4:00 *Thomas Jefferson Describes his "Novel Techniques"*
for Unearthing the Mysteries of the Past
(Ms. M-C. Garden and Mr. B. Barker)

4:20 *Comments by our Discussant* (Mr. M. Brown)

Critical Acclaim for Storytellers I (Corpus Christi):
"Most of the audience stayed... awake" — *AAA NEWSLETTER*
"We were amused. 3 stars!" ··· *QUEEN VICTORIA, Empress of India*
"That's nice, dear." -- *Mr. PRAETZELLIS'S MOTHER*

Two sides of the playbill issued to the audience at the 1998 Society for Historical Archaeology conference. The performers played to a packed house.

was described as a weaving together of "evidence archaeological, documentary, pictorial, and imagined to create first-person stories." Her stories began with Nathanial Tracy who, failing to

THE PERFORMANCES

SLAVES, RINGS, AND RUBBISH
Martin Hall

Narrator ....*Martin Hall*

LOST MEMOIR OF A LOWELL BOARDINGHOUSE KEEPER
Mary C. Beaudry

Miss Martha A. Peasbody (A Reform Advocate), reading the words of Mrs. Amanda Fox.........................*Mary Beaudry*

FORT FREDERICA'S HIDDEN PAST, OR TALES A POT MIGHT TELL
Anne Yentsch

Old Pot...................................*Anne Yentsch*
Gen. Ogelthorpe.........*Nicholas Honnerkamp*
Loyal Son....................*Howard Morrisson, III*
Lab director...............................*Jud Kratzer*

"I Never Expect to Preach There Again."
Rowdy Times in a 19th Century Virginia River Town
Robin L. Ryder

John Early (A Circuit Preacher), Personae
....*Robin Ryder*

RED LIGHT VOICES: DIALOGUES ON PROSTITUTION, CA. 1900
Julia G. Costello & Judy Tordoff

ACT I: Men Talk
Rene (An Upper-Class Brothel Customer)
....*Julia Costello*
Lew (A RR Worker and Frequent Brothel Customer)..........................*Judy Tordoff*

(RED LIGHT VOICES continued)

ACT II: The Life
Lola (A Parlor House Prostitute from the Dominican Republic)...............*Judy Tordoff*
Maimie (An Independent Prostitute)
....*Julia Costello*
ACT III: Family Business
Violet (Born in a Brothel, She Entered the Family Business)...................*Julia Costello*
Marc (A Successful Pimp).......*Judy Tordoff*

PLANTATION DIALOGS: A CONVERSATION IN ONE ACT AND TWO CENTURIES
Dan Mouer & Ywone Edwards-Ingram

Auntie Molly, Jane, Prof. Roberta Marley
.............................*Ywone Edwards-Ingram*
Captain Pleasant (aka "Massa"), Dick, Prof. P.C. Liberal.........................*Dan Mouer*
The Voice of Passing Time and Personnae
....*James Ingram*
Robin Ryder will serve as Sound Engineer

THE TALE OF FERMIN VALENZUELA
Adrian & Mary Praetzellis

Narrator (A UC Berkeley-educated Lawyer) and Postmaster......................*Robin Ryder*
Fermin "Frank" Valenzuela (Teamster and Cattle Rustler) ....*Dan Mouer*

THOMAS JEFFERSON DESCRIBES HIS "NOVEL TECHNIQUES" FOR UNEARTHING THE PAST
Mary-Catherine Garden & Bill Barker

Colonial Williamsburg Archaeologist
.............................*Mary Catherine Garden*
Mr. Thomas Jefferson............ ....*Bill Barker*
Tour Participants.....................*The Audience*

get anywhere in politics, spent his years improving his farm. The last was sickly Sarah Broadman who reflects on married life and finds solace in her needlework and flower garden.

In *Bread Fresh from the Oven* Julia Costello used the words of Italian immigrants and their descendants who built and used stone bread ovens in the foothills of California's Sierra Nevada range. *"They didn't have a recipe..."* recalled Flossie Sabatini (b. 1914). *"It was made by memory; by hand; by the feel of it. And the crust part! We all fought for that first crust piece. Oh that was good!"*

The *Lurid Tales and Homely Stories of New York's Notorious Five Points* told by Rebecca Yamin contrast how nineteenth-century writers portrayed the place with the "homely" insights into the lives of individuals offered by archaeology. Five Points was not merely the slum home of degraded people, as it was portrayed in earlier accounts and the movie *Gangs of New York*. The Goldbergs were observant Jews whose household discards showed their religious observance. Nearby, the resident of a brothel whose fancy tableware showed how clients were entertained and the remains of whose baby also found their way into the refuse pit. These were real people with complicated lives.

The *Archaeologists as Storytellers* franchise is, by the way, open for anyone to claim.

If Ruth Tringham had been part of one of the Storytellers companies (unfortunately she wasn't), her presentation would have overwhelmed the rest of us. If the flat pages of this book could have done justice to her work, I would have devoted this section to it. Ruth's multimedia constructions are some of the most transgressive and downright interesting offerings in archaeology today. Her presentations involve sight and sound: images of people, archaeological excavation in process, reconstructed sites, text, objects, as well as music and voice. Her work pushes the boundaries of the archaeological imagination by recombining fragments from the process of archaeological excavation, highly complex, the results of scientific studies of things like plant phytoliths, and imaginative vignettes of her own creation. Like many artistic performances, Ruth's work is to be experienced, not written about and dissected.

The theatricality of Tringham's presentations emphasizes that these are artificial constructions. This draws our attention to how separate archaeologists are from our subjects as subjects, but how close as humans. Run one these presentations (see "Things to Read" at the end of this chapter) but don't just ask yourself, "What am I supposed to get out of this?" Experience it for the WOW as well as for insights into the past.

Do transgressive archaeologies belong in a book about 'theory'? After all, they don't offer a perspective on human history or culture like social theories do. Yes, they do, and here's why. Every one of the ideas in this book began with an act of creativity. Then an archaeologist applied a theory to the situation and the data through a second act of ingenuity. Transgressive approaches unlock the archaeological imagination that makes that step possible by helping us to see possibilities outside the familiar academic divisions.

The sum up

Many archaeologists are skeptical about all this.

The responses to transgressive performances at archaeological conferences range from puzzlement to joy, from thoughtful to grumpy. The supremely dismissive proclaim that the mode is acceptable for outreach to the *public*. Indeed, the distinction between public and professional products is fully institutionalized and is actually codified in the government regulations that control **CRM**. Never the twain shall meet. More than one young university teacher has been advised to steer clear of the whole alternative mode for fear peers will brand her a lightweight.

The most worrying criticism of this approach will continue to be that fiction and other interpretive accounts allow us to present our vision of a plausible past without the inconvenience of explaining how we got there. One legacy of the New Archeology is the necessity to be explicit about our methods and assumptions. This is a good idea and you'll not see me abandoning it. However, some kinds of insights are simply not amenable to that approach. Transgressive archaeologies don't necessarily throw out the scientific approach, or not all of it. Their aim is to get at different ways of understanding and to use the ambiguity of what we do to inspire and stimulate.

127

Transgressive approaches make holes in the barrier between work that's considered scholarly and the rest, but they don't demolish the boundary entirely. Archaeologist James Deetz used to say that John Barth's postmodern-ish novel, *The Sot Weed Factor*, brought him closer to life in colonial America than most archaeology. I doubt he would have said the same of archaeological pop fiction like Jean Auel's bestseller, *The Clan of the Cave Bear*.

Questions to Discuss

Is the text/artifact analogy useful in archaeology? Or is it taken too far? How useful is Bathes's pleasure/jouissance distinction?

Are artifacts multivocal? If they are, then is there no end to the ways we can interpret them? And can no interpretation be said to be 'wrong'? Where does that leave archaeology as a scientific discipline?

Respond to the critique that transgressive approaches simply take the easy way instead of doing the hard intellectual work of archaeological interpretation.

If this kind of work became popular, might the field lose its credibility, as the public could no longer tell fact from fiction?

Is this presentation style mere self-indulgence? After all, what's so bad about the standard academic conference structure? Where do you draw the line between scholarship and art?

Should archaeologists engage with interpreters of the past from outside the academy? And if they do, won't it legitimize baseless, nonscientific speculations? Would you share the stage with proponents of alternative ('aliens built the pyramids') archaeologies?

Things to Read

Auel, Jean
1980 *The Clan of the Cave Bear.* Crown Books, New York.

Barth, John
1960 *The Sot Weed Factor.* Doubleday, New York.

Barthes, Roland
1977 The Death of the Author. Pages 142–148 in *Image-Music-Text.* Translated by Stephen Heath. Hill & Wang, New York.

Beaudry, Mary
1998 Farm Journal: First Person, Four Voices. *Historical Archaeology* 32(1):20–33.

Costello, Julia G.
1998 Bread Fresh from the Oven. *Historical Archaeology* 32(1):66–73.

Danto, Arthur
2013 *What Art Is.* Yale University Press, New Haven, Connecticut.

Joyce, James
2000 *Ulysses.* Penguin Books, London.

Praetzellis, Mary (Ed.)
1998 Archaeologists as Storytellers. *Historical Archaeology* 32(1).

Tringham, Ruth
2010 Forgetting and Remembering the Digital Experience and Digital Data. Chapter 4 in *Archaeology and Memory*, Dusan Boric (Ed.). Oxbow Books, Oxford, UK.
2013 Pivoting and Jumping through the Fabric of Catalhoyuk to an Imagined World of People with Faces, Histories,

Voices, and Stories to Tell. Presentation at the
Engendering Landscape and Landscaping Gender conference, University of Buffalo. tinyurl.com/Tringham-
show (accessed September 2014).

Yamin, Rebecca
1998 Lurid Tales and Homely Stories of New York's Notorious
Five Points. *Historical Archaeology* 32(1):74–85.

CHAPTER 11
ARCHAEOLOGICAL BIOGRAPHY

When it comes to the past, everyone writes fiction.

Stephen King

Anthropological theoreticians preaching the overriding importance of behavior patterns [may] spawn a contempt for the more traditional archaeologists who seek knowledge about one place, one man, or one moment.

Ivor Noel Hume

What is archaeological biography?

Archaeological biography is the study of individuals, families, and households using the methods of archaeology. OK, so what if I just made that up? We authors get to do that. But in spite of the fact that it's not a widely used term, archaeological biography is commonly practiced under various guises and as part of various theoretical frameworks.

Archaeological Theory in a Nutshell: Adrian Praetzellis, 133–142.

Archaeological biography springs from a couple of basic principles:

1. All archaeological sites are created by events and processes that occur in historical time: a woman chips out a stone tool; a fire destroys a wooden building; then a flood buries the 'site' under a layer of sediment.
2. Because all sites consist of the material remains of events like these, first and foremost they reflect things that happened at particular places and times, and to the people who lived and worked there.

Furthermore, the educated reader will not be surprised to learn that

1. Many (although not all) archaeologists self-identify as anthropologists.
2. Anthropologists have historically been less concerned with the lives and experiences of individuals than of groups.

The end result is this: Although all archaeological excavations initially reveal the results of small-scale events, many archaeologists would rather use these data to say things about large-scale processes. We didn't, of course, develop this inclination spontaneously, and to explain quite how it came about you'll have to delve into the history of the field as it was practiced in North America, as I've explained in Chapter 1.

If only Lewis Binford had enjoyed reading French, things might have turned out differently... for while the New Archeologists were getting all hot under their lab coats about the necessity to generalize, philosophers like **Michel Foucault** were arguing the reverse: that universal truths don't exist, that the search for them is an illusion, and that decoding texts (or artifacts) requires local knowledge. At the same time **Clifford Geertz** began to apply some of these ideas to ethnography. The result was the method he called **"thick description,"** which emphasizes the close interpretation of individual acts at the small scale.

And if you think this is starting to sound like a method for archaeological biography, you're right.

Archaeological biography and archaeology

Some of the earliest archaeological work done in North America presages what I'm calling archaeological biography. James Hall excavated the Massachusetts home of Miles Standish, one of the original Mayflower settlers, in 1853. Later, in the 1880s, the citizens of Sacramento, California, set out to preserve the

Faceless blobs. Is this how you think of the people of the past? It's hard to conceive of people as individuals who lived so long ago and had lives that, on the surface, were so very different than ours. And then archaeology comes along... (Thanks to Ruth Tringham, and apologies to Pieter Bruegel the Elder.)

disintegrating remains of John Sutter's fort and to dig up portions of it that were no longer extant. It's likely that Hall wanted to memorialize his iconic ancestor, while the local worthies of Sacramento were ready to see their own 50-year past as History.

Of course, it isn't necessary to lionize the people of the past in order to prevent them from being **"faceless blobs,"** people whose lives are of no interest to archaeologists except in the aggregate. In rescuing our predecessors from this kind of oblivion archaeological biography refocuses on a past populated by individuals, people whose lives changed throughout their life courses in ways that were both structured and predictable (going through the phases of childhood, adolescence, parenthood, and so on) and subject to the vagaries of historical chance and individual **agency**. Since most people live their lives in families and households, it makes sense to study the history and culture of their era at that scale. Working at this level also gives us access to a gendered archaeology, since male and female relations are often played out at the household scale.

Archaeological biography tries to unravel the influences of important historical and cultural processes at particular places and times, and to show how these influences affected the lives of the specific people whose artifacts we handle.

An example of archaeological biography[1]

Like many archaeologists, Anne Yentsch didn't choose the Calvert site as much as it chose her—or was chosen for her by circumstance. The site was scheduled for destruction by a development project when Yentsch and her colleagues took their first look. Ironically, the very forces of destruction that brought the site to her attention provided the opportunity to dig it up.

"It was an "incredibly rich site," she tells us. And this is a significant phrase, for by "rich" Yentsch doesn't just mean that it contained lots of artifacts and features but also that its interpretation "stretches the imagination" of the archaeologist.

---

1 Anne Yentsch, *A Chesapeake Family and Their Slaves* (1994).

This statement foreshadows Yentsch's creative approach to the archaeology of this place. But I'm getting ahead of myself.

The site in question (and at imminent risk from the bulldozer) was the home of the Calvert family. In the 300 years since the house was constructed, the town of Annapolis, Maryland, had built up around the family estate, most of which had long since been subdivided and sold off. This semi-rural complex was now in the center of town. Although other settlers had occupied the land before their arrival in 1727, the archaeological site mostly reflected the Calverts. Yentsch calls the place a family compound. It housed as many as three generations of Calverts, miscellaneous cousins, and other hangers-on. It was also home to as many as 30 East African-born slaves and their children.

The Calverts were as close to a hereditary aristocracy as you could find in colonial America. Five generations of the family served as Governor of Maryland in the seventeenth and eighteenth centuries. They were wealthy tobacco growers and titled English nobility. The archaeology mainly reflects the 1727 to 1734 residence of Captain Charles Calvert and that of Benedict and Rebecca Calvert, who lived there from 1748 to 1788.

Archaeologists love people who are prolific builders and are also untidy enough to leave plenty of evidence of their everyday life hanging around. Fortunately for Yentsch, Captain Calvert was both. "Englishmen," she writes, "achieved social status, in part, by ostentation." The captain was a good example of this dictum. Archaeology shows that the captain built several additions to the family home in his short tenure, including a formal garden and an orangery heated by a sophisticated under-floor system. The similarity between this feature and the hypocaust that warmed the baths of the ancient Roman aristocracy would not have been lost on Calvert's classically educated contemporaries. As governor of Maryland, the captain had to continuously reaffirm his status so as to stay ahead of political rivals. So improvements like these were as much symbolic structures intended to impress the visitor as they were utilitarian ones.

Portrait of two boys, Charles Calvert and an unnamed slave by John Hesselius (1761). Although relatively little of their skin shows, there's no doubt who's the little heir and who the servant. The modern viewer may be left wondering the name and history of the other boy. For eighteenth century whites, he was merely a prop.

Yentsch moves seamlessly between archaeology, historic records, art, and ethnography. Is she a historian? An anthropologist? A biographer? She is certainly a humanist, taking pleasure in juxtaposing the portrait of Rebecca Calvert as a child with an archaeologically discovered wooden block painted with the letter B. Elsewhere, she compares two Calvert probates (lists of possessions compiled after the owner's death) with those of the region as a whole to make the point that the family was on the cutting edge of Annapolis society as far as the possession of modern household goods (for example, table forks and mattresses) were concerned. The social ritual of "hospitable drinking" is well represented in the Calvert family's archaeological remains: there are far more serving vessels of prestigious and expensive Chinese porcelain in the Calverts' archaeological collection than on other contemporary sites. You can easily imagine the captain using these cups and plates as props in a performance to impress the region's worthies.

The captain's daughter, Rebecca, eventually married her cousin, Benedict Calvert, but this loyalist family's influence was in decline and their material remains show how they responded to the change. From the archaeology it's clear that Benedict remade the formal European garden into a working yard with stable and smokehouse; the terraces were buried under fill, and the orangery was demolished. As Yentsch puts it, the landscape took on a more conventionally Maryland appearance, conforming to local practices and aesthetics rather than leading them.

The sum up

Some scholars see insights into the small scale—the home, children, individual lives—as trivial in the Long Run and irrelevant in understanding the Big Picture. Historian **Fernand Braudel** famously wrote that observations at this level were merely the "foam on the wave" of historical process. In response, I point out that only *species* exist in the Big Picture because (to quote John Maynard Keynes) "in the Long Run we're all dead anyway."

Anne Yentsch's portrait of a Chesapeake family beautifully bridges the gap between the small and large scales. Yet much of mainstream archaeology still has little time for what it considers particularistic studies of the lives of individuals and households. This is partly due to the anthropological interest in groups and partly because archaeologists have not come to terms with the emotions that come to the fore when we get involved with past lives and touch the very objects that 'our' people touched.

Consider this: Many of our archaeological predecessors were antiquarians who sought nifty artifacts to admire, display, and generally pore over in the comfort of their Victorian parlors. For them, it was all about the aesthetic and exotic qualities of the item itself. From the casual pocketer of conveniently unattended arrowheads to the professional treasure hunter, modern day artifact collectors have similar goals, and archaeologists are keen to separate themselves from these folk. As a field, archaeology is unwilling to admit that artifacts may appeal to us aesthetically and that archaeologists don't renounce our roles as social scientists when we have an emotional reaction to these objects and connect with their former owners as human beings.

Questions to Discuss

Why do archaeological biographers place so much emphasis on context? Can one do archaeological biography without archival documents? Could you do it for a prehistoric person/family?

To what degree do you conceive of the people of the past as "faceless blobs"? Is that inevitable unless we run the risk of projecting our own emotions and motivations into an unknown past?

What insights can archaeological biography give into gender, class, and social roles in the past?

What would the New Archeologists have thought of archaeological biography? Can we learn anything about general cultural/historical processes from the method or is it all about glorifying the individual?

Might the emphasis on individual agency and romantic detail that's inherent in archaeological biography lead us to downplay the role of social structures?

Is archaeological biography closer to historical particularism or Geertz's thick description?

Things to Read

Braudel, Fernand

1995 *A History of Civilizations*. Translated by Richard Mayne. Penguin Books, Harmondsworth, UK.

Flannery, Kent

1973 Archaeology with a Capital S. In Charles Redmond (Ed.), *Research and Theory in Current Archaeology* (pp. 47–53). Wiley-Interscience, New York.

Geertz, Clifford

1975 *The Interpretation of Culture*. Basic Books, New York.

Keynes, J. Maynard

2007 *The General Theory of Employment, Interest, and Money*. Palgrave MacMillan, London.

Noël Hume, Ivor

2010 *A Passion for the Past: The Odyssey of a Transatlantic Archaeologist*. University of Virginia Press, Charlottesville.

White, Carolyn (Ed.)

2009 *The Materiality of Individuality: Archaeological Studies of Individual Lives*. Springer Press, New York.

Yentsch, Anne

1994 *A Chesapeake Family and Their Slaves*. Cambridge University Press, Cambridge, UK.

CHAPTER 12

PHENOMENOLOGY

We know not through our intellect
but through our experience.

Maurice Merleau-Ponty

What is phenomenology?

Phenomenology is the study of subjective human experience. Its goal is to know the world as other people do. In archaeology, it is used to figure out how people felt through their senses what are now archaeological sites but used to be populated places. That anyone would seriously try to get inside the heads of long dead others may sound like the flakiest of self-delusions. But persevere. There's a lot more to it.

Back in seventeenth century Europe, philosopher **René Descartes** was trying to work out the relationship between thought and action—between what we think and what we do. We have, says he, minds and bodies. Emotions, beliefs, and values are things of the mind; they don't have actual physical

Archaeological Theory in a Nutshell: Adrian Praetzellis, 143–154.

existence. And then there's the material world of things that take up space. They have mass, weight, color, can be hot or cold, and so on—like your body.

An event in the material world creates a mental reaction that leads to an instruction to the body that results in the body taking action. You see a plate of crispy onion rings. You desire it. Your mind instructs you to take one. Your hand reaches out and grabs it. And that, concludes Descartes, is how we know the mind rules the body. Ta da! This seems to make sense and to account for everything quite comfortably. Exit the philosopher feeling pretty good about himself.

But if it were that simple I wouldn't have written this book, and Descartes's model didn't satisfy everyone. Fast forward to the 1940s, and Maurice Merleau-Ponty points out that the mind isn't just influenced by raw information coming in from the senses (that onion ring smell). Contrary to what Descartes thought, people don't experience things directly but through a whole wad of filters set up by their culture, their own perceptions, and their experiences of the world.

Pierre Bourdieu called this complex of cultural filters and experiences "**habitus**." The word sounds like 'habit,' and for good reason. Habitus is composed of all the routines of people's everyday lives together with the norms and shared beliefs of the society in which they live—what anthropologists would call their culture. In fact, culture is passed on through these routines of life until the whole thing becomes second nature. We recognize someone's social status without having to be told what it is. We know our own relationship to them and how that should translate into appropriate behavior, and we follow through on that knowledge. For the very reason that these things 'go without saying,' they are as obvious to us as how to get to the nearest post office. Habitus is a useful idea because it links the actions and perceptions of daily life with cultural practices.

I started off saying that phenomenologists want to express how people experience life through their bodies. As Merleau-Ponty pointed out, embodied experiences are not merely a matter of rational response to sensory input. People experience their surroundings by processing sensory input through lenses influenced by habitus. Walking along a familiar trail one might recall events that are said to have happened there. And having expectations about what may be around the corner will influence our actions and bodily response. If I walk the same path a lot I may fall into a habituated, self-reinforcing response.

Of course, the *particular* lived experience will depend on the individual, be she an adult woman, disabled man, and so on. Yet the fact that he or she *has* an experience is the result of living in a physical body and its habitus-influenced responses. This idea is central to understanding how people of the past experienced their world.

Phenomenology and archaeology

Archaeology is about the relationship between people and their artifacts. Phenomenology fits in at the actual places where these lived experiences, these relationships, happened. Much archaeology that uses a phenomenological approach is done at the scale of culturally formed landscapes in order to work out how people in the past experienced these big artifacts. Several early phenomenological studies were done of massive European Neolithic monuments of rock and earth (ever heard of Stonehenge?).

It's no accident that many of these awe-inspiring 5,000 plus-year-old constructions are within an easy drive of the University of Oxford, in southern England, where archaeology and phenomenology came together in the 1980s. These structures have an impact on the senses of any observer who isn't an emotional block of wood. And it's easy to imagine how that stimulated pioneers like Chris Tilley to feel that scientific descriptions were missing something by concentrating on measureable characteristics. Instead, said he to himself, wouldn't it be good to think about how Neolithic people *felt* about these structures?

Tilley and his fellow Oxfordians were on the same track as old Maurice Merleau-Ponty. He pointed out that empirical

Stonehenge. Looking N.E. from the altar stone towards the hele stone.

Stonehenge by Heywood Sumner (1916).

disciplines (like archaeology) tend to assume that attributes that can be measured have more reality than sensory, experiential information—that quantifiable data are 'hard' whereas sensory information is 'soft.' Consequently, archaeologists had usually studied landscapes by making plans and cross sections, by measuring things and comparing them: this henge is X feet in diameter whereas that one is Y feet. This **etic** approach takes the view of the disinterested outsider. It is basic to the scientific method, which wants verifiable observations (facts) to make controlled comparisons.

But wait just a minute, says the phenomenologist. Where is it written that size was more important than color or position on the landscape to the people who used and experienced these structures?

This **emic** or insider approach is key to the phenomenological method. Every artifact has multiple qualities: size, color, shape, location, relationship to other artifacts, and so forth. That New Zealand's Maori people have 3,000 words for "red" (according to Merleau-Ponty) shows that the redness of an object is not perceived to be separate from the categories of the object itself: it's not a "flower that happens to be red" but a "redflower." So rather than chop the attributes of a Neolithic landscape up into digestible chunks of data, the phenomenological approach looks at them as wholes in the same way, we assume, as the people who experienced the monuments in the deep past did.

Archaeologists are now delving into senses other than sight to think about how the people of the past experienced their world. A pioneer in the field of auditory archaeology, Steve Mills mapped a post-medieval mining landscape in rural Cornwall, UK, using GIS technology to figure out the place of the sounds of mining in the past as well as what happened when this industrial activity stopped. And he did something similar with a nineteenth-century British railway station, which goes to show what happens when you let your imagination loose.

But people in the past didn't just experience landscapes, they did things there. Social anthropologist Tim Ingold came up with the word "taskscape" to capture the idea that the meaning people attach to places comes from the activities, both routine and special, they do there. A taskscape is a time and place within which people put social relations, artifacts (broadly defined), and ideologies into practice.

The relationship between phenomenology and other archaeologies is analogous to the development of Method Acting—yes, acting as in the theatre. Until the late nineteenth century actors were taught technique. They learned how to project the

147

voice, how to stand, and how to make recognizable gestures to convey the usual emotions. Put these techniques together and, voilà!, you're acting. Then the Method came along and actors were taught to draw upon their own senses and emotions in the context of the plot to empathize with their characters and express their feelings. Phenomenology can be problem-oriented in the same way as conventional archaeology. Its distinctiveness is in its method, which involves achieving empathy by taking the position of the participant.

An example of phenomenological archaeology[1]

About 7,500 years ago a group of adventurers left Sicily. They sailed about 55 miles south across the Mediterranean, ran into the Maltese Islands, and settled there. Time passed, and for a couple of millennia Maltese culture seems to have been similar to that of the old country, Sicily and southern Italy. Then, some 5,600 years ago the Maltese started to build temples, around 30 in all, and continued doing so for about 1,000 years.

Although the most obvious reason to build a temple is to deal with the gods, religion has as many roles in society now as in the past. Chris Tilley thinks that constructing and using the temples was one way the Maltese people separated themselves culturally from their neighboring ancestral lands. It was part of how they actively developed and maintained a distinctive Maltese identity. As John Robb puts it, "The Maltese didn't live on an island. They built themselves one."

Ḥaġar Qim (pronounced something like *had-jar keem*) is a hilltop temple complex that overlooks the rugged coast of southern Malta. Tilley describes it as "poised between the heavens and the sky and the depths of the sea." It was extensively redesigned and rebuilt during its 1,000-year life, creating a maze of passages, rooms, and side niches that would have been disorienting to its lay users. Tilley speculates that it was used for rites having to do with agriculture, human fertility,

1 Christopher Tilley, *The Materiality of Stone* (2004).

At Ħaġar Qim, Malta. A man peers through an opening into the temple, unsure if he should enter. Phenomenologists have looked at how the act of negotiating one's way through the temple's passages and halls may have affected users' experience of this building.

initiation into various social ranks and statuses, and treatment of the dead. He conceives of it as a complex performance space where religious specialists created a sensory environment to manipulate the experience of participants in ritual events. How Tilley figures out the design and the effectiveness of this priestly choreography is an absorbing and masterful example of phenomenology in action.

Where a standard architectural description might provide a room-by-room description of dimensions and construction details, Tilley describes his own passage through the sequence of spaces as a participant may have done. He explains the effects as he encounters them: an opening allows a view of the cliffs;

the necessity to crawl from one room to another; a space that could be seen but not entered; the "oracle holes" through which items might be passed.

Since he experienced the temple spaces himself, Tilley could describe how his body (and by extension, the bodies of ritual participants) reacted to this carefully manipulated environment through

> forcing changes in physical bodily posture [standing, stooping, crawling]... changes in volume [voluminous vs. narrow]... changing effects of light and the amplification of smell and sound... tactile impressions [smooth and rough surfaces]... manipulation of perspective [inability to judge distance]... special visual effects through [artificial] light and sunlight, art and decoration.

The disorienting effect of this maze-like environment was made even more bewildering by the priests' ability to block and open various rooms and doorways at will. The space never had to be the same twice; surprise was constant. In this way, priests directed the emotional responses of participants, impressing on them how the rituals at Ħaġar Qim allowed access to an extra-ordinary, super-natural reality. That these rituals were only available to Maltese would have strengthened their identity as a people.

The sum up

Tilley structured his description in the same way social scientists usually report on their work. He began with some history, went on to describe his idea, presented his data, and came to a conclusion. But I have a feeling that the actual process was not so linear. Crawling through the temple remains in a phenomenological frame of mind may (I speculate) have stimulated his imagination to see the connections between what he had read, conversations with colleagues, site history, ethnography, archaeology, and his sensory experience. I mention this because real world archaeology is as **inductive** as it is **deductive**.

What constitutes data for the phenomenologist? Conventional archaeologists don't have a problem identifying facts when they see them. That there were 66 pieces of yellow ware in Context 2-143 is easy to document and put on a graph. But although environmental perceptions are the phenomenologist's stock in trade, they are culture-specific. Was darkness necessarily scary and dangerous to all groups of people at all times in the past? Perhaps a cave was thought of a place of concealment and safety. Can we be sure that Neolithic farmers had the same reactions to their environment as an Oxford Ph.D. doing his summer fieldwork?

I tried to find a good example of phenomenological analysis in historical archaeology. No luck. Perhaps this is because the wealth of archival documentation makes us think we already understand the people of the recent past. Tilley has at least one advantage over historical archaeologists: everyone who experienced Ħaġar Qim is dead. They can't contradict him, and they left no documents that others might use to poke holes in his ideas. At the end of the day, the problem many people have with phenomenology is knowing how to evaluate its results. We judge the validity of conventional science by examining the data and how they are analyzed. But if two people looked at the same landscape and came up with different interpretations it might be hard to know which one (if either) you should believe. As that's true of conventional archaeology, how much more so in areas where the 'hard data' don't appear to be quite as solid?

That said, the charge that these unconventional accounts of the past are closer to creative writing than scholarship is unfair to people like Chris Tilley. For although they don't document their conclusions in the usual way, they do show how they got there.

Questions to Discuss

How is the idea of "habitus" that different from "culture"?

What is meant by 'soft' and 'hard' data? Which do you feel more comfortable working with? Do qualitative data seem less 'real' than quantitative data?

What do you think of the analogy between Maori language and Neolithic perception? Is it acceptable to make this kind of cultural and chronological jump?

What is an 'embodied experience'?

What is the relationship between phenomenology and empathy?

Can we be sure that the bodily experience of the modern archaeologist evokes similar responses to people who lived millennia ago? That is, can the phenomenologists' insights into the past be verified?

Is describing the lived experience of people in the past a legitimate research goal?

Things to Read

Bourdieu, Pierre
1990 *The Logic of Practice*. Translated by Richard Nice. Stanford University Press, Stanford, California.

Descartes, René
1995 *The Philosophical Writings of Descartes*. Translated by J. Cottingham, R. Stoothoff, A. Kenny, and D. Murdoch. Cambridge University Press, Cambridge, UK.

Hoskins, W. G.
1955 *The Making of the English Landscape*. Hodder & Stroughton, London.

Ingold, Timothy
1993 The Temporality of the Landscape. *World Archaeology* 25(2):152–174.

Merleau-Ponty, Maurice
2013 *Phenomenology of Perception*. Translated by Donald Landes. Routledge Books, London.

Mills, Steven
2014 *Auditory Archaeology: Understanding Sound and Hearing in the Past*. Left Coast Press, Inc., Walnut Creek, California.

Robb, John
2001 Island identities: Ritual, travel and the creation of difference in Neolithic Malta. *European Journal of Archaeology* 4(2):175–202.

Skeates, Robin
2010 *An Archaeology of the Senses: Prehistoric Malta*. Oxford University Press, Oxford, UK.

Tilley, Christopher

2004 *The Materiality of Stone: Explorations in Landscape Phenomenology*. Berg, Oxford, UK.

CHAPTER 13
MATERIALITY AND THING THEORY

The Medium is the Message.

Marshall McCluhan

Who ever heard of a door mat TELLING anyone anything?
They simply don't do it. They are not that sort at all.

Mr. Mole, *The Wind in the Willows*

What is materiality?

Materiality is a way of thinking about things/objects that recognizes that they aren't just tools used by people to achieve
human ends. Things actively influence society and culture.

Like several of the ideas in this book, materiality isn't so
much a 'theory' in the scientific sense as it is a frame of reference—a different way of looking at a familiar subject.
Archaeologists are comfortable with the idea that people make
and use artifacts to get stuff done. But the notion that things in

---

Archaeological Theory in a Nutshell: Adrian Praetzellis, 155–165.

turn create us is relatively new. As a way of thinking, materiality is less concerned with what people want to achieve with things than the **agency** of things themselves.

You may have noticed that I'm using the word 'thing' rather than the common archaeological term 'artifact' or 'material culture.' That is intentional because materiality is not only concerned with those categories but with everything in the material world that can be perceived by our senses. **Artifacts** are things created by people. It's a useful concept but a rather static one. The idea of **material culture** presupposes that artifacts can be 'read' by understanding how they are made, used, and disposed of (see Chapter 10). Again, it's a useful term but limited.

Materiality refers to the relationship between people and all kinds of things, artifacts or not: trees, fog, apples, the smell of rain, as well as the human body itself, its color, height/weight ratio, and eventually its level of decay. Materiality has a phenomenological concern with how texture, color, smell, sound, mass, and so on were perceived by past societies (see Chapter 12). But more than this, materiality seeks to understand how, for example, the qualities of a particular type of rock were symbols to the people that used it in certain ways. How things (not just artifacts) came to represent the unspoken ideas that people infused into them.

And how do things come to embody particular values? Here we must go back to our friend **Pierre Bourdieu**'s idea of **habitus** (I wrote about it in Chapter 12)—the way people are enculturated into their society and how they form concepts (such as death) with reference to the things that are part of their group's environment. Shapes, colors, and other sensory characteristics come to represent ideas. Memories that are attached to things underpin habitus. In this way, humans create things that in turn create us as social beings as they shape our thought patterns.

The material world, the world of things, is around us from birth, so we take it for granted. It is mundane, and we don't give it a second or even a first thought. This is why conceptual art is effective. Andy Warhol's famous lithograph of a Campbell's soup can is effective (and worth millions) because it surprises us. We don't expect an ordinary soup can to be the subject of 'art.' It's just something that sits on the shelf with rows of other identical things. But Warhol pulled it from the background and made it a subject in itself.

This distinction between things as members of groups of things (a shelf of soup cans) and an **object** (a particular soup can separated out for special attention) is the basis of something called **Thing Theory**. And, yes, that is really what it's called. Things are just there. We hardly even notice them. But as soon as we set a particular object apart we become conscious of it and it becomes understandable.

Is it a thing or an object? That depends on the cultural context of the viewer. To me that hill in the distance is just a lump on the horizon. But to the knowledgeable traditional person it's the body of a supernatural beast. A smooth green rock is only one thing among many until it is intentionally positioned and becomes a funeral monument, an object. In this way the qualities of smoothness and greenness become infused in a cultural concept of death. They become part of and reinforce habitus.

Consequently, studies that use the idea of materiality must reconstruct past emic categories of things, as you'll see in the example of the stone monuments of Rapa Nui (Easter Island) that follows in a couple of pages.

Materiality and archaeology

As I write this early in 2014, archaeologists are busy spring cleaning their research agendas, tidying away antiquated terms like 'material culture,' and eagerly pulling shiny new concepts out of the box for display to our peers. Materiality is the current buzzword in archaeology. Who knows what the catchphrase will be when you read this.

In the scramble for up-to-the-minuteness the term is sometimes stretched past its useful meaning. So let's get this straight: materiality isn't materials science. Technology may come into it, but there's more to it than that. Similarly, we shouldn't confuse materiality with **materialism**—the desire to acquire things. **Marx** was interested in things as commodities and wanted to show what stuff can be made to do (see Chapter 3). He was not (as far as I'm aware) interested in the 'thinginess' of things themselves.

The recognition of habitus as a creator of cultural distinctiveness was preceded by the theories of late nineteenth century archaeologists such as Gustaf Kossina. His idea was that cultural traits and their associated artifact patterns were "bred into the bone" of particular cultural groups. "Sharply defined archaeological cultural areas," wrote Kossina, "correspond unquestionably with the areas of particular people or tribes." Different "**races**," it was claimed, had inborn proclivities towards certain attitudes and behavioral traits. The idea turned ugly as it was co-opted into the ideology of racial superiority and culminated in the Nazi death camps.

For decades, archaeologists retreated into the reconstruction of historical events and processes and the creation of regional artifact typologies, chronologies, and other empirically based work. The New Archeology turned this around in the search for universal commonalities—cultural processes that are not limited to particular times and places. Later, the postprocessual movement emphasized how people use the symbolic power of artifacts to achieve particular social and political goals. Significantly, many postprocessualists saw the carriers of these symbols as entirely arbitrary. The artifacts themselves (the things) were unimportant except as the bearers of the message (see Chapter 1).

And so now we arrive at materiality, which archaeologists picked up in the 1990s on cross-campus visits to their colleagues in art and material culture studies. At the time, many archaeologists were still busy figuring out what artifacts did (their utilitarian, social, and adaptive functions) and when and where they did it (their chronology). Materiality turned the question around, Chris Gosden famously asking, "What do objects want?" Now, things don't have *intention* of course, but they do function as actors in human social life. They aren't just passive lumps.

An example of materiality-inspired archaeology1

The carved stone heads of Rapa Nui (Easter Island) are so huge in size (as much as thirteen feet tall) and unexpected in location that some people think they were created by extraterrestrials. Although that's nonsense, their existence does require some explanation because Rapa Nui is a long way off the bus routes.

The island is about 2,100 miles west of Chile in the South Pacific and about 1,200 miles from its nearest neighbor to the east. This supremely isolated spot was settled by Polynesians who travelled there in canoes 800 or 1,000 years ago, depending whom you ask. It's a small place, just over 60 square miles, but may have had a population of as many as 6,000. Descendants of the original settlers still live there, although in very reduced numbers.

The famous stone heads (*moai*) rest on stone platforms (*ahu*) and were in place by about the year 1200. In addition to these constructions there are a great number of canoe-shaped houses (*hare paenga*), ovens (*umu*), rock-walled gardens (*manavai*), quarries, and roads throughout the island. Most of the *moai* were carved in a volcanic crater, Rano Raraku, while the statues' eight-foot-tall 'hats' (*pukao*) and the *ahu* were made of a different stone entirely. This porous red lava was quarried several miles away at a place called Puna Pau.

Archaeologist Sue Hamilton of University College London has been studying Rapa Nui since 2007. Earlier work focused on unraveling what some call the Mystery of Easter Island. These questions were primarily historical and **processual**: how the *moai* were made and transported, the structure of Rapa Nui society, and the processes that led to the 'collapse' of this society of builders. But Hamilton's team (and archaeologists almost always work in teams) is taking a more **hermeneutic** approach.

---

1 Sue Hamilton, *Rapa Nui (Easter Island's) Stone Worlds* (2012).

Two of the massive stone heads, *moai,* on Rapa Nui (Easter Island).

Rather than looking for the answers to specific questions about what happened here, she is trying to get an "island-wide understanding" by looking at the system of quarries and roads that brought the *moai* to their resting places.

And why is Hamilton's approach different from all other approaches? Where earlier workers looked at quarries and saw places where stone was cut, Hamilton found evidence that linked them to the *moais'* final destinations. While earlier workers interpreted *moai* sitting by the side of roads as 'abandoned,' Hamilton's research indicates that they were intentionally placed there. She put quarries and roads together as elements of a sacred landscape that linked the place of production to the place of installation.

Some of this evidence of a continuous sacred landscape is in the form of eyes carved into the walls of the red rock quarry at Puna Pau. Of course, only living things have eyes, and Polynesian tradition has it that this stone replenishes itself, like other living things. The eyes at the beginning of the road have their mates at the ocean end. These *moai*, surmounted by their red stone 'hats' and sitting on their red stone plinths, are set up facing inland, toward their source. Their eyes seem to have been made of obsidian and coral.

The design of the ocean-side structures is like this: The *ahu* platforms have their backs toward the ocean. On the ocean side of the *ahu* are cremated human remains. The *moai*, which are believed to depict ancestors, face inland and toward a stone-surfaced plaza where rituals may have been carried out. Now, in Polynesian cosmology the souls of the dead travel across the ocean to the origin point of the ancestors. These structures fit into this cosmological scheme and can be taken as visual metaphors for the relationship between the realms of the living and the dead. They are places of transition where dangerous boundaries are defined and ritually managed.

But didn't the people of Rapa Nui simply use whatever building material was readily available in ways their technology would allow? The insight of materiality makes us dissatisfied with this kind of functionalist explanation. To look at the materiality of Rapa Nui is to seek understand how the builders converted stone into physical depictions of ideas and cosmologies. It looks at the significance of their choices in the creation of these metaphors of belief and thought.

The Rapa Nui project combines the approaches of phenomenology and materiality. From the former comes the realization that the people of the past constructed sensory environments as the settings to enhance their experience of the sacred. The materiality of the scene draws our attention to the culturally significant redness of the *pukao* and *ahu* stones; the towering *moai* with their coral and obsidian eyes; and the ocean side setting with its sights, sounds, and smells, so different from the inland. A road is not merely a way of transporting things from one place to another. It is part of a memory-building system

161

by which the journey of the *moai* and red *pukao* and *ahu* stones contributed memories to the features that continued after they were in place.

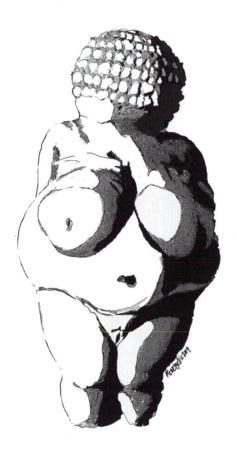

The "Venus of Willendorf." Was this piece of Paleolithic sculpture a depiction of a deity, an objectified sex symbol, or possibly even a self-portrait of a pregnant woman?

The sum up

As a practical matter, materiality won't supersede conventional research domains. People will always want to know who did what they did and when they did it. And that's OK because a materiality perspective isn't something that most of us will take on separately from other approaches. You can't take the materiality of life, put it on a table, and dissect it like a frog in the bio lab. The whole point is that things are irretrievably bound up with everything we do and think.

Considering the materiality of a situation expands our ability to understand what things meant to their users. Stuff has a reflexive relationship with its creators, and the split between the material (things) and mental (thought) is found to be artificial, an invention.

The perspective of materiality contends that things stand for ideas. But in the application of this principle it's still up to someone to figure out which things and which ideas. That's where the archaeological imagination comes in—such as Timothy Taylor's inspired account of "Why the **Venus of Willendorf** has no face." Taylor rethought the time-honored 'mother goddess' idea and concluded that the Paleolithic 'Venus' figurines may not have been goddesses or pregnant women's self-portraits— but rather depictions of a *category* of beings. With no face but intricately carved and exaggerated breasts and genitals, she is a female but not a person. So, rather than representing a time when women were venerated as the source of life, these figurines may be the earliest examples of sexual **objectification**. Thanks for the uplifting thought, Tim.

Questions to Discuss

What's the difference between the concepts artifact, material culture, and 'thing'? Are these differences, if any, useful or just more academic hairsplitting?

Can you have agency without intention? Do things *really* have agency?

How does memory affect meaning? How could material qualities come to represent ideas and attitudes? And how can you figure out what the ideas were?

How is materiality different from taking a symbolic approach to the meaning of things? Are they mutually exclusive? What other research approaches might be happily united with materiality?

How is Sue Hamilton's work at Rapa Nui an example of hermeneutic interpretation? Come to think of it, what is hermeneutics?

Things to Read

Brown, Bill
2001 Thing Theory. *Critical Inquiry* 28(1):1–22.

Godsen, Chris
2005 "What do objects want?" *Journal of Archaeological Method and Theory* 12(3):193–211.

Grahame, Kenneth
1908 *The Wind in the Willows*. Methuen, London.

Hamilton, Sue
2012 Rapa Nui (Easter Island's) Stone Worlds. *Archaeology International* 16:96–109.

Klein, Leo
1999 Gustav Kossinna, 1858–1931. In Tim Murray (Ed.,) *Encyclopedia of Archaeology* (pp. 233–246). ABC-CLIO Books, Santa Barbara, California.

McCluhan, Marshall
1967 *The Medium Is the Message*. Penguin Books, Harmondsworth, UK.

Taylor, Timothy
2006 Why the Venus of Willendorf Has No Face. *Archäologie Österreichs* 17(1):26–29.

CHAPTER 14

THE NEXT BIG THING, OR WHERE DO WE GO FROM HERE?

I take it too seriously to take it literally.

Rabbi Michael Aaron Robinson

Where we came from and where we are now

The tale of how the goals of archaeology (in North America, at least) changed from the reconstruction of culture histories to whatever they are now is a familiar one. We are in yet another period of change so it's a good idea to learn from the past. If archaeologists can't do that we really are in trouble.

Some conventional histories of archaeological thought present the rise of the New Archeology as a paradigm shift—a profound reorientation of how archaeologists thought about what they did and how they did it: And lo, the prophet Lewis Binford arose and spread the Holy Word of Science. Immediately, or pretty damned fast, he gathered a following of believers and the old ways were swept away. Time passes, the new prophet Hodder arrives from over the ocean bringing

Archaeological Theory in a Nutshell: Adrian Praetzellis, 167–177.
© 2015 Left Coast Press, Inc. All rights reserved.

the teachings of the postprocessual deity, and the process is repeated.

Sounds rather simplistic? How right you are.

John Bintliff has pointed out that this account has been told and retold so often that it has become a creation story with its own sets of ancestors who, in turn, are overthrown in Oedipal frenzy by their successors. The reality was different because these were actually slow processes that individual archaeologists bought into at different rates, and some not at all. Furthermore, says Bintliff, this model doesn't reflect what most archaeologists actually did. Rather than throwing off everything that went before and taking up the theoretical model of the moment, many archaeologists would actually pick and choose from the new options depending on how this or that might work at their site, like items on a menu.

Whether or not archaeology underwent a paradigm shift, it certainly experienced what David Clarke called a "loss of innocence." Although Clarke described this process way back in 1973, it may be the single most important influence on the way archaeologists think and is why archaeological theory looks like it does today. The rather simple relationships that archaeologists had, in their innocence, assumed existed between collections of artifacts and archaeologically defined 'cultures' did not hold up to scrutiny. In fact, the way in which one should interpret archaeological data became problematized rather than something archaeologists took for granted. From this seed of dissatisfaction grew the many 'isms' I described in earlier chapters.

I've retold this old story because if you believe in the archaeological creation myth, you may think we're overdue for another paradigm shift. Some say that the postprocessual era has had its day. Perhaps even theory itself won't survive.

Will *that* be the Next Big Thing?

The death of theory?

Not so long ago two archaeological conferences offered this question: Are we experiencing or should we encourage the

death of theory in archaeology? The titles of these conferences, which I will talk about in a few seconds, were devised to get people to talk about the state of theory. No one proposed that we don't need no stinkin' theory—just the opposite—but they did have things to say about the future.

The organizers of the original *Death of Theory?* Session, held in 2006 in Poland, wanted to assess whether archaeology may be better off without "unitary theoretical paradigms." The session's title was derived from Roland Barthe's famous death-of-the-author announcement (see Chapter 10). If that proclamation allowed literary scholars the freedom to go beyond the author's intent in interpreting his or her words, might the same benefits accrue to archaeology without the tyranny of research approaches that currently tend to dominate? The organizers weren't interested in discussing the merit of one theory versus another but with the culture of archaeologists that sometimes turns theory into ideology. The result, says John Bintliff, is that *my* idea is considered a legitimate topic for scholarship, but *yours* isn't. More about this later.

The Theoretical Archaeology Group (TAG) was created as a venue for people to talk about theory at a time (1977) when it was on everyone's mind. Although mostly a British thing and very successful, the organizers of the 2009 conference came up with the *Death of Theory* theme in part to spark controversy. Everyone had heard about the session in Poland, though hardly anyone knew anything about it aside from the title, which some completely misunderstood and consequently became quite huffy. The TAG bosses also wanted to deal with the worrying trend that theory was becoming less prominent at TAG conferences. Lynn Meskell disagreed with the premise, at least in relation to North America. There, said she, theory was alive and well.

Years ago, Brian Fagan wrote that archaeology's "dirty little secret" was the number of unreported excavations. Here's another one that is discussed as contributing to the potential Death of Theory: the commercialization of archaeology.

It's estimated that as much as 90 percent of archaeological investigations in the United States are done by non-academicians to fulfill some legal requirement or other. In many ways this is quite different from the kind of archaeology done by your average professor and written up in scholarly articles. Within certain practical limits, academicians generally decide for themselves what problems they want to investigate, where they want to work, and on what schedule. Few commercial archaeologists have those freedoms. Their projects are partite, which means they can't usually carry a research agenda over to the next site. They also have to satisfy government regulators who simply won't accept many of the 'isms' presented in this book as having the potential to yield important information. As a result, much commercial archaeology and, therefore, many practicing archaeologists use theory in a formulaic way, as window dressing. (Author's note: I'll get reamed for that comment but what the hey.)

Of course, there are exceptions to this depressing picture. Many commercial archaeologists do highly respected, theoretically informed, and innovative work that is cited in the scholarly literature and has wide currency. And countries such as France have avoided commercialization entirely. But I believe that for most people on most days the reality is something different. Since the government and commercial sectors employ most archaeologists in less than ideal conditions, I think that the Next Big Thing may lead theory in a more pragmatic direction.

The Next Big Thing

Having come this far, or even having just skipped to the end, the reader may feel entitled to know how it will all turn out. Archaeologists have been batting the theory ball around for decades now, and you might think it reasonable to wonder if they won't soon come to some conclusion. Well, I'm going to make a prediction about that: **There will be no Next Big Thing**.

You read it here first, and I'll buy you a $10 beer at the conference hotel bar if I'm wrong.

No doubt there are plenty of 'isms' waiting to be born. Approaches like Ian Hodder's **entanglement** (which I can't possibly explain here) will probably come along and gather some into their particular folds, but I'm not talking about that. Everything I've learned about archaeology makes me believe that archaeologists as a group will never cozy up to a unifying theory or paradigm the way biologists have to evolution. In spite of what our origin myths say, archaeologists didn't fall in line for processual archaeology or for what came after, and there's no reason to believe that's going to change.

So what *will* theory look like in the post-Big Thing era? As Jacquetta Hawkes famously wrote, "Every age has the Stonehenge it deserves—or desires." Each period comes up with solutions that are acceptable in the zeitgeist of the time, and right now archaeology seems to be ready to take advantage of the insights of previous years rather than either running onwards to embrace the next 'ism' or circling the wagons around a particular research agenda. The future will (I hope) be increasingly pragmatic and aware of the needs of real archaeologists struggling to make sense of real sites. What might that look like? Read on...

Revisit the past and rummage in the toolbox

Mark Pluciennik has written that academia "tends to valorise the new" at the expense of existing models. Some of these older ideas were imported from other disciplines and slapped onto archaeological studies with insufficient thought about how they may relate to *archaeological* data, as distinct from those of sociology or art history. I've done it myself so I know it's true. Nobody wants inertia, but an intellectual culture of constant change is wasteful of good ideas rejected for no better reason than that they've apparently passed their sell-by date.

So the post-Big Thing may involve revisiting some of the approaches (like those in this book) taken up and almost immediately set down again as the next shiny idea came into view.

Most of this book has been a fairly linear compendium of concepts and theories. Reading it from beginning to end one might come away with the idea that each of these approaches lives in its own house and doesn't talk to the neighbors. According to Mark Pearce, what is needed is a type of theoretical cherry picking. He believes that many archaeologists have for years sampled from an *à la carte* menu of theoretical possibilities like those I've written about, selecting the dish (approach) that is to their taste (need) at the time.

Pearce and his colleague John Bintliff suggest we use any device in the theoretical toolbox that seems to fit. In this way, the archaeologist can come at a problem from any number of theoretical stances instead of decorating one favored model with archaeological data like ornaments on a Christmas tree. They call this approach **bricolage** and feel that it is not only a more realistic strategy than the unified alternative but more accurately represents what real archaeologists actually do. As Maria Mayan points out, one should choose one's tools (methods and approaches) to fit the job (research need) at hand.

Another emerging approach that is similar to the call for cherry-picking in its practicality has been suggested by Timothy Pauketat. He contrasts the scientific investigation of the ultimate causes of things (via, for example, neo-Darwinism) with the approach of history, which is more concerned with the interconnectedness of events and immediate agency. Pauketat's "historical processualism" suggests that social and cultural change (aka, history) can be understood by studying change at a variety of scales, from the household to whole societies. He suggests that figuring out *how* things happened is a more achievable goal than speculating about *why*. Like Pearce and Bintliff, Pauketat believes that archaeology can be rigorous without being so single-minded as to delegitimize other ways of seeing.

These proposals have a lot of potential. They reflect what archaeologists actually do—to make sense of the information that real sites throw at them—rather than what others say they should be doing in some greater cause. Research issues are often still derived from larger theoretical models, but one isn't limited in what that model should be. From the dirt archaeologist's perspective, this makes them adaptable to a variety of sites and the types of archaeological data these sites produce. From the perspective of the consumer (the public, other archaeologists, historians) what they produce are much more readable, human-centered accounts because they are grounded in action and agency.

Think of ethnogenesis. Archaeologists can investigate it as a process and come up with scientific generalizations about the conditions under which it occurs and so forth. On the other hand, it happened to real people under real conditions of life. And archaeology is in a great position to figure out how the process was reflected in and created by their daily decisions.

Together with the kind of pluralism that we see in modern archaeology there is also a tendency to separate into hostile camps. Certain well-known academic departments of anthropology are deeply divided between those committed to the hard sciences and those whose approach is more ethnographic. Let's hope archaeology isn't on the way to becoming, in the words of Rabbi Jonathan Sacks, "self-selecting congregations of the like-minded" instead of maintaining a conversation based on our common heritage.

These suggestions won't make everyone happy in Archaeologyland. In general, people who are committed to evolutionary and interpretive archaeologies haven't been able to find common ground, and these modest proposals won't bridge that gap (although as my publisher, Mitch Allen, pointed out "we got a book on that"). And there are legitimate reasons to be concerned if the field as a whole were to turn in the direction of bricolage. Some would like to see a field that is more focused on the answers to the big questions that face humanity, such as environmental change. Focusing on local places and local experience, they warn, may become the pursuit of the trivial.

I don't know the answer, but I admire the question.

Questions to Discuss

What does the Death of Theory mean?

Is there such a thing as an atheoretical archaeology? If so, what does it look like?

Might archaeologists' flirtation with postmodern uncertainty undermine our field's traditional authority over the past and how it is interpreted? Would that be a good thing? Who or what would replace our authority? (A self-created, self-edited, self-authenticated Wikipedia model perhaps?)

Is there strength in a diversity of orientations and goals, or is the more single-minded approach of normal science a better model for archaeology? Will superficiality be the result of a short archaeological attention span in which every minor issue is given its fifteen minutes of fame?

Do different types of questions about the past require different approaches? If so, will archaeologists ever agree that it is important to study certain Big Issues for the benefit of humanity as a whole?

What might those Big Issues be?

Things to Read

Bintliff, John and Mark Pearce (Eds.)
2011 *The Death of Archaeological Theory?* Oxbow Books, Oxford, UK.

Clarke, David L.
1973 Archaeology: The loss of innocence. *Antiquity* 47:6–18.

Cochrane, Ethan and Andrew Gardner (Eds.)
2011 *Evolutionary and Interpretive Archaeologies: A Dialog.* Left Coast Press, Inc., Walnut Creek, California.

Fagan, Brian
1996 Archaeology's Dirty Little Secret. *Archaeology* 48(4):14–16.

Flannery, Kent V.
1982 The Golden Marshalltown: A Parable for the Archeology of the 1980s. *American Anthropologist* 84(2):265–278.

Hawkes, Jacquetta
1967 God in the Machine. *Antiquity* 41(163):174–180.

Hodder, Ian
2012 *Entangled: An Archaeology of the Relationships between Humans and Things.* John Wiley & Sons, West Sussex, UK.

Kintigh, Keith, Jeffrey Altshul, Mary Beaudry, Robert Drennan, Ann Kinzig, Timothy Kohler, Frederick Limp, Herbert Maschner, William Michener, Timothy Pauketat, Peter Peregrine, Jeremy Sabloff, Tony Wilkinson, Henry Wright, and Melinda Zeder
2014 Grand Challenges for Archaeology. *American Antiquity.* 79(1):4–24.

Mayan, Maria J.

2009 *Essentials of Qualitative Inquiry.* Left Coast Press, Inc., Walnut Creek, California.

Pauketat, Timothy

2001 Practice and History in Archaeology: An Emerging Paradigm. *Anthropological Theory* 1:73–98.

Pearce, Mark

2011 Have Rumours of the 'Death of Theory' been Exaggerated? In John Bintliff and Mark Pearce (Eds.), *The Death of Archaeological Theory?* (pp. 80–89). Oxbow Books, Oxford, UK.

Pluciennik, Mark

2011 Theory, Fashion, Culture. In John Bintliff and Mark Pearce (Eds.), *The Death of Archaeological Theory?* (pp. 31–47). Oxbow Books, Oxford, UK.

Praetzellis, Adrian

2011 CRM Archaeology: The View from California. In Chris Gosden (Ed.), *The Oxford Handbook of Global Archaeology* (pp. 319–331). Oxford University Press, Oxford, UK.

Theoretical Archaeology Group (TAG)

2009 Abstract Book. The 31st Annual Meeting of the Theoretical Archaeology Group. Department of Archaeology, Durham University, Durham, UK.

CHAPTER 15

PARLEZ-VOUS PO-MO? A MOSTLY POSTMODERN PHRASEBOOK

All these abstract ideas are enough to make a poor student's head explode. And as if archaeo-lingo wasn't enough, the would-be archaeologist must also contend with concepts from *outside* our discipline that are now in fairly common use by our colleagues. Many derive from fields such as literary criticism, art history, and communication studies, as well as social and political theory.

But fear not.

It occurred to me that the occasional reader (not *you* of course) might not recall the difference between the ideas of **Derrida** and **Barthes** or how to pronounce **Foucault** [foo-*coh*]. And the same individual might be apprehensive about, for example, slogging through **Gramsci**'s *Prison Notebooks* (1971) to understand what the old fellow meant by **cultural hegemony**.

So I did it for you! In fact, all the words in **boldface** are in this phrasebook.

Here I offer explanations in mostly ordinary English of some terms of postmodern **discourse** (including that word)

Archaeological Theory in a Nutshell: Adrian Praetzellis, 179–200.

that are used a lot in postprocessual archaeology, as well as more general archaeology stuff that I hope is useful. Sounds good, eh? But beware. A lot of these ideas are self-referential: to understand one term you may have to look up another. And how anthropological archaeologists use these terms may only scratch the surface of their meanings in other disciplines. Since this is an *archaeological* lexicon, mine are working definitions based on how archaeologists use the terms, and not even all archaeologists.

By its nature, **postmodernism** disallows definitively authoritative definitions of anything, so if you think I got it wrong, blame the discourse. Just don't ask for your money back.

Agency. The idea that individuals are the active creators of their own lives, rather than the powerless pawns of forces they can't influence. This interest in human agency was a response to Marx and the structuralists who saw history as a series of structural changes in which individuals are interchangeable actors playing predetermined roles. (see **Marx** & Chap. 3, **Structuralism** & Chap. 8, **Poststructuralism, Practice theory**)

Althusser, Louis. (*loo-*ee *al*thu-sair). French philosopher who came up with the idea that states develop both repressive ways of maintaining power (such as the police and the army) and ideological ones (like religion and the judicial system). While the former "apparatuses" (his word) force people into conformity, the latter are more insidious because their job is to make the dominant ideology seem rational and legitimate. In this way, the ruling class governs with the consent and even the support of the very people they subordinate. Althusser was a Marxist. But you already knew that. (see Chap. 4)

The Archaeologist's Guide to Sandwich Making

Author's Guide, Society for American Archaeology: "While diversity of breads is encouraged and preference may be given to multigrains of non-bleached flour origin, no slice may exceed 12.7 x 10.16 cms (5 by 4 ins)."

Lewis Binford: "As I told Griffin in 1948, a sandwich that contains no pickle is not a sandwich at all and has no business calling itself one."

James Deetz: "As Henry Glassie (1975:43) points out, the bilateral symmetry of bread/filling/bread exemplifies a structure that is also present in architecture and gravestone design."

Ian Hodder: "We must involve all stakeholders, both producers and consumers, in the process of sandwich-making. The Catal Hyuk website presents the ingredients with their original grocery bags to encourage multivocal approaches to this imaginative process."

Stanley South: Egg Salad Pattern

Bread	35.4%
Egg	24.1%
Mayonnaise	17.4%
Onion	14.9%
Celery	08.2%
	(100%)

Ivor Noel Hume: "Ladies should be discouraged from pursuing this craft, for long fingernails may leave holes in the bread. They may, however, do the washing up."

Randall McGuire: "The question is who makes the sandwich? And for whose benefit? The functionalist contention that the sole purpose of sandwich production is to provide food ignores its role in social reproduction."

Carmel Schrire: "While the sandwich is essentially an artifact of conquest whose origins lay in the parlors of the English elite, the meaning of this square and ordered form was subtly transformed by a ragged slice of wildebeest or gnu."

Janet Spector: "Many stories may be reconstructed (or constructed) regarding how sandwiches were made. What, I wonder, might s/he (the maker) think of my interpretation? Of my sandwich?"

Allison Wylie: "Beginning with explicit definitions of the subject matter—such as Binford's (1962) ethnoarchaeology of the BLT—the New Archeologists went on to question basic assumptions of previous practice: Is bread truly a diagnostic characteristic (Clarke 1972:43) and must it 'sandwich,' so to speak, a filling (Watson et al. 1971:17)?" characteristic (Clarke 1972:43) and must it 'sandwich,' so to speak, a filling (Watson et al. 1971:17)?"

Annales school. A type of historiography (the writing of history) that emphasizes the large, long-term processes that underlie the laundry list of historical events recounted by traditional narrative histories. These underlying influences (economic, social, environmental, and so forth) were famously described as the wave on whose crest is generated the foam of particular events and the famous people who supposedly willed them into being. The Annales approach sees history as the result of long-term patterned behavior structured by cultural and natural forces rather than a series of events coordinated by and for important individuals. This resonated with anthropologically trained archaeologists who saw the Annales historians as soul buddies. (see **Fernand Braudel**)

Artifact. Something made or modified by humans. (see **Material Culture**)

Barthes, Roland (ro-*lond* baart). French (you knew that was coming) literary critic who came up with the idea that readers participate in the process of creating the meaning of texts. Barthes died after being run down by a laundry truck. (see **Death of the Author** & Chap. 11)

Braudel, Fernand (fare-*nond* bro-del). Leading light of the **Annales** school of history. Hardly necessary to say that he was French.

Bricolage (*briko*-largj). As a method, bricolage uses concepts and methods from a variety of apparently unconnected sources to create a theory, narrative, explanation, or work of art. Originally used by Claude Lévi-Strauss to describe how traditional stories are assembled from a mosaic of cultural sources. (see Chap. 14)

CE. Common Era. An alternative way of referring to dates used instead of the conventional AD (*Anno Domini*/Year of our Lord). The equivalent of BC (Before Christ) is BCE (Before

Common Era). The system avoids referencing events in the Christian calendar.

Context. Where things (objects, ideas, events) stand in relation to time, space, and culture. The *stratigraphic* context of an artifact is its physical relationship to other objects and archaeological structures. Its *historical* context includes what people thought of it and how they used it. Context is everything you need to know to understand the meaning of something.

CRM. Cultural Resources Management.

Cultural ecology. A school of thought based on the premise that culture (any culture) is an adaption to the particular environment in which it developed. Many **New Archeologists** took up this approach in order to generalize about human society and culture. (see Chap. 1 & 2)

Cultural relativity. The idea that one can only understand a culture in relation to its own system of beliefs and customs. It doesn't follow that I have to approve of every cruel practice because it is or was 'their culture.' But I must suspend my judgment temporarily to examine the case.

Culture history. Descriptions of past societies based on their **material culture** that employ artifact typologies and similar tools to figure out their chronologies and geographical ranges. (see Chap. 1)

Death of the Author. The French equivalent of 'huh?' was probably uttered when **Roland Barthes** first declared that authors aren't responsible for their own books. The inevitable response—"OK then, Monsieur Smart-Arse, who *did* write *Les Miserables*?"—would have missed the point. He didn't mean that they don't personally thump away at typewriters (this was 1977); of course they do. His point was that the reader has an active role in interpreting meaning that may have little to do with what the author had in mind. In what may have been intended as an unambiguous statement, the reader may see layers of meaning of which the author is not aware but that are, nevertheless, parts of the message being communicated.

Deconstruction. One of the key methods in the postmodern project to destabilize meaning. The method is used to show that every piece of text, picture, and object has multiple levels of meaning, from the plain meaning of the words to their hidden implications. (see **Jacques Derrida** & Chap. 1 & 7)

Deduction. Part of the scientific approach that involves testing the validity of a hypothesis. The deductive method begins with ideas about the world rather than with observations (data). (see **Induction** & Chap. 1)

Derrida, Jacques (jhak *derry*-da). Another French postmodernist. This gent came up with the idea of **deconstruction**.

de Saussure, Ferdinand (fare-*nond* duh so-soor). French linguist whose ideas about the structure of language are the basis of **structuralism**. (see Chap. 8)

Descartes, René (ren-*ney* day-*cart*). French seventeenth-century philosopher who concluded that the mind (thought) rules the body (the material world). (see Chap. 12)

Determinism. In social theory, the idea that a particular factor 'determines' the course of history, the structure of society, and so on. For example, some forms of **Marxism** are deterministic because they contend that history is the result of class conflict. (see Chap. 3 & 4)

Direct historical approach. This important method in North American prehistory involves using ethnographic and ethono-historic information about extant cultural groups to make inferences about the peoples who preceded them. (see Chap 1)

Discourse. The unspoken rules by which groups of people (such as politicians and professors) and disciplines (like archaeology) think and communicate. If you can 'control the discourse' you decide what it is acceptable to think and say on a topic. A concept dreamed up by the ever power-obsessed **Michel Foucault.** (see Chap. 1 & 7)

Doxa. Ideas that are so set in our minds that they 'go without saying.' (see **Ideology** & Chap. 9)

Empiricist. One who believes only what can be directly observed. Often the same people who claim that the 'facts speak for themselves,' who don't need theory, and who won't buy this book. (see Chap. 1)

Epistemology. The study of how we know what we think we know—what separates a gut-level belief from justifiable opinion. (see Chap. 1)

Essentialism. The idea that groups of humans (men, women, or people of certain ethnicities) have proclivities or attitudes that are inescapable parts of their 'essence': for example, men are innately outgoing because of their evolutionary history as breadwinners, whereas women are passive due to the needs of childraising. It's what people mean when they say 'human nature.' Needless to say, some folk don't care for this kind of stereotyping since it is used to rationalize excluding them from full participation in society. Our friend **Jean-Paul Sartre**'s philosophy of existentialism was built around rejecting this idea. (see Chap. 7)

Faceless blobs. A term devised by Ruth Tringham to describe the apparent anonymity of people in the distant past. She uses archaeology to return their humanity to people long dead. (see Chap. 5 & 11)

False consciousness. A popular and firmly held illusion about reality that tends to stabilize the status quo in society. **Marx's** view of religion as the "opium of the masses" expresses the idea that it's in the interest of those in authority to convince their social inferiors that they'll get their reward in Heaven. (see **Ideology** & Chap. 3)

Feminism, first wave. The initial phase of feminist activism in the modern Western world. Began in the late eighteenth century with the goal of achieving basic equality under the law and culminated with the right to vote. (see Chap. 6)

Feminism, second wave. Building on the achievements of the first wave, the women's rights movement of the 1960s and '70s emphasized women's legal autonomy over their own bodies (for example, abortion and contraception) and eliminating androcentric practices that prevented women from participating on an equal footing with men at work and in society at large. (see Chap. 6)

Feminism, third wave. Heavily influenced by postmodern theory, this development of the 1980s and later emphasizes not only the gender issues of the earlier waves but takes in **postcolonial** theory, elements of **Marxism, poststructuralism**, and other heavy and somewhat abstract notions. More of an academic/intellectual movement than a popular one. (see Chap. 3, 5 & 6)

Foodways. Everything that contributes to how people obtain, prepare, serve, and consume food. Using bowls rather than plates and chopping meat into chunks rather than eating it off the bone are aspects of foodways. As eating stew involves bowls not plates, archaeologists sometimes hypothesize how people prepared their dinner based on their pots. (see Chap. 9)

Foucault, Michel (me-*shel* foo-*coh*). One of that band of deceased French philosophers whom I place in the category 'greatly influential but largely indigestible.' He wanted to show how society defines deviance in order to control what is considered normal and acceptable. He enjoyed playing with kittens and **deconstructing** concepts like madness and punishment. Foucault's central interest was in power: who has it and how they got and keep it. I made up the part about kittens. (see **Discourse** & Chap. 7)

Front-end loading. The process whereby an author lards the beginning of his or her article with references to up-to-the-minute social theory that are never mentioned again in order to demonstrate their erudition. I learned this term from Marley Brown, who may have been its creator. (see Chap. 1)

Functionalism. A mechanical view of human society based on analogy between cultural practices and institutions and the way the parts of the body work together to sustain life. Although the premise is correct, useful even, it's a rather rigid model of viewing the very complicated human 'organism' and has problems accounting for change. (see Chap. 1, 3, 9 & 12)

Geertz, Clifford. Anthropologist who came up with the concept of **thick description**. (see Chap. 11 & 14)

Gender. A cultural construct that corresponds to, but is not the same as, biological sex. While individuals' sex is a matter of their biological characteristics (most people are either male or female), their gender is ascribed by their culture. Along with this comes a whole string of deeply rooted assumptions about the appropriate roles of males and females in society which, because they correspond with biological sex, appear 'natural.' **Feminism** and **queer theory** want to challenge and change these assumptions. (see Chap. 6 & 7)

Gramsci, Antonio. Author of writings on power and **hegemony** called *The Prison Notebooks*, which he drafted while... in prison. (see Chap. 4)

Great Chain of Being. A medieval model of the hierarchical relationship of all beings to each other. At the top is God. Below are angels, the king, nobility, the common people, all the way down to animals and rocks. The order was seen as fixed and immutable. If you were born a peasant, that was God's intention and you should stay there. You don't have to be a **Marxist** to realize how convenient this was for those towards the top of the list. (see **ideology, false consciousness** & Chap. 3)

Habitus. French sociologist Pierre Bourdieu uses the word to mean all the attitudes, categories, and unconscious practices that everyone acquires in the process of growing up in a particular place and time. Interpretive archaeologists use the term a lot because the meaning one assigns to an **artifact** or an experience is based in one's habitus. (see Chap. 8 & 12)

Hegemony (heh-*jem*ony). The constant threat of violence is an inefficient way of getting people to do what you want because when individuals comply they don't feel that they are being 'good,' only pragmatic. It's better by far to let the population police themselves by convincing them that what *they* want happens to be what *you* want, too. And that it's just common sense to think that way. (see **Antonio Gramsci** & Chap. 4)

Hermeneutics. Originally used to describe various approaches to understand the Bible, it now refers to methods of interpretation in general. Hermeneutics assumes that the meaning(s) of a thing (such as an artifact) is not intrinsic—it is not just sitting there waiting to be discovered. Interpretation is an active process by which people give things their meanings. In a hermeneutic approach, new understandings are continually being generated. Ian Hodder calls this process the "hermeneutic spiral" and describes how the present understanding of an object builds on previous interpretations in a continuous progression. (see Chap. 1 & 12)

Heteronormal. The uncritical assumption that heterosexuality can be taken as historically **normative**. **Queer theory** has **problematized** this position. (see **LGBT** & Chap. 7)

Historical materialism. A view favored by Marx's buddy Friedrich Engels in which the events of human history are seen to result from the material conditions of life, notably power relations between social classes. This view gives agency to history (things didn't just happen) and has clear political implications. (see **Marxism, materialism** & Chap. 3)

Historicism. In its simplest sense the word means to understand an object or text in the historical context of its creation. Some Marxists use the term in a pejorative sense, pointing out that to accept the assumptions about reality by uncritical past thinkers is to be a sort of accomplice to class oppression. Yes, it's a politically loaded term. (see Chap. 1)

Horizon. An artifact type (such as the arrow point) or assemblage of types that appear rapidly across a region.

Idealism. The belief that thoughts and ideas precede and are more important than actions. It is the antithesis of **materialism**. (see Chap. 3)

Ideology. Marx and Engels wrote that "the ideas of the ruling class are in every epoch the ruling ideas." By "ruling ideas" they meant the mindsets that people take for granted as common sense and don't think to challenge. These are their ideologies. (see **False Consciousness, Marxism** & Chap. 4)

Indeterminacy. Presenting multiple interpretations without the attitude that one is 'right' while the others are 'wrong.' (see Chap. 1)

Induction. Accumulating information, observing patterns, and then coming up with an explanation that accounts for what you've observed. Induction is the reverse of **deduction**. In practice, archaeologists tend to use both methods. (see Chap. 1)

Jouissance (*jhoo*-ee-sonse). Our friend **Roland Barthes** contrasts *jouissance* ('bliss') with **pleasure**. We get simple pleasure from comfortable practices such as viewing representational art or reading unambiguous prose. *Jouissance* is the disconcerting yet thrilling experience we have in the unfamiliar that turns our assumptions on their heads. Trying to read James Joyce's book *Ulysses* is both unsettling and stimulating because it goes against everything we expect a book to be like. Listening to atonal music provokes a similar experience. (see **Readerly/Writerly**, **Transgressive** & Chap. 10)

Lévi-Strauss, Claude (clood *leyve*-strohs). French anthropologist who championed **structuralism** as a way to understand human societies. L-S was interested in the universals of human thought and thought that cultural practices can only be understood by getting at the structures that underlie them. These structures really exist as far as L-S in concerned; they aren't just heuristic devices or metaphors. His book, *The Savage Mind*, attacked the old prejudice that so-called primitive peoples are child-like in their thought processes. L-S would say that they are structured in the same way as everyone else. (see Chap. 8)

LGBTQ. Acronym for lesbian, gay, bisexual, transgender. The purpose of adding Q for **queer** or questioning to the mix is to recognize non-**heteronormal** identities. (see Chap. 7)

Liminal. In social anthropology lingo, a person is in a liminal state when he or she is teetering between one social condition and another. For example, in some Western cultures, teenagers are considered neither adults nor children; they have neither the freedom of the former nor the responsibility of the latter. **Postcolonial** analyses use the term to bring out the arbitrary nature of binary social categories: colonizer/colonized, masculine/feminine, white/colored, and concepts such as **heteronormality.** (see Chap. 5)

Longue durée (long dur-*ray*). The idea, as practiced by **Fernand Braudel,** that long term events and processes (such as climate and geography) have a greater effect on what we call history than definable events like wars and political maneuverings. (see **Annales school**)

Marxism. According to Karl Marx and his buddy Freidrich Engels, history is the result of conflict between social classes. They saw all modern society and philosophy as mechanisms by which those in power stay there. Although Marx saw revolution as the inevitable end result of history, you don't have to be in favor of revolution to see the value of his ideas in understanding how societies work. Some archaeologists who want to distance themselves from Marx's revolutionary politics while holding onto some of his social theories call themselves materialists. (see **Historical Materialism, Materialism** & Chap. 3)

Material culture. Not just a synonym for **artifact**, this concept incorporates the idea that things are cultural creations and consequently have meaning apart from their utilitarian purpose. (see Chap. 4 & 13)

Materialism. The idea that the material conditions of life determine how we see the world, rather than the reverse. For example, materialists think that religious **ideologies** emerge from how power is distributed in society rather than creating the society through their ideas. Materialism contrasts with the vision of a subjective reality made up ideas and perceptions, **idealism.** Samuel Johnson famously dismissed the latter idea by kicking a rock and remarking, "I refute it thus!" (see **Great Chain of Being, Historical Materialism, Marxism** & Chap. 3)

Metanarrative. A story about the past that explains the present. The colonizer's vision of an unoccupied wilderness that is put to its best use by settlement is a metanarrative that helps make history understandable and coherent through a convenient generalization. As a story, metanarrative will fit the facts but must discount variability as anomalous. It lays behind the interpretation of facts, providing a framework to understanding. (see **Postmodernism** & Chap. 1)

Modernism. This concept has little to do with being modern in the sense of up to date. It's the way of thinking that has dominated the West for the last couple of centuries, emphasizing human advancement through science and logical decision-making rather than looking to religion and received wisdom ('rationalism over revelation'). Capitalism is the dominant political **ideology** of the modern era. (see **Postmodernism** & Chap. 1)

Multivocality. The quality of having multiple meanings. An archaeological journal article that includes, for example, interpretations from both the scientific and descendant communities is said to be multivocal. (see Chap. 4 & 11)

New Archeology. A movement of mostly North American archaeologists that emphasized using the scientific method and quantification to study cultural processes. The New Archeologists wanted to know why things happened, not just what, where, and when. I have left out the second 'a' in the word archeology in keeping with the practice of the New Archeologists who saw it as a symbol of European intellectual **hegemony.** (see **Postprocessual** & Chap. 1, 2, 13 & 14)

Normal science. The process by which scientists use the accepted methods of their field to investigate research issues.

Normative. A view that assumes all members of a society are aware of and conform to their group's cultural norms. In archaeology, it conveys the idea that these norms are embodied in a group's artifacts. (see Chap. 1, 8 & 9)

Objectify. To dehumanize another person or group by recognizing only their sexual characteristics (breasts, for example) or supposed racial/ethic features, such as skin color or hair type. Objectifying people makes it easy to rationalize all types of callous acts because, after all, they're not like fully human you and me. They are in fact, **Other.** (see Chap. 12)

Other. Always defined from the standpoint of the observer and often given a capital letter, the Other consist of members of **objectified** groups. **Postcolonial** theory stresses how a dominant group's definition of Other bolsters its claim to mastery. If an imperial power defines the 'natives' as childlike and unable to govern themselves, then it's only right to lend them a hand. Rudyard Kipling's phrase "the White man's burden" refers to this imperial attitude toward the Other. (see Chap. 2 & 5)

Pleasure. The comfortable feeling we get from reading an uncomplicated book or viewing a univocal piece of art. These are **readerly** works. (see **Jouissance** & Chap. 10)

Post-. Whenever you see the prefix 'post-' (meaning *after*) you can tell that the concept involves a critique of some familiar concept. It's a **postmodern** thing.

Postcolonialism. An intellectual and political movement concerned with the historical, cultural, ideological effects of colonialism by (mostly) European nations from the seventeenth century onward. Postcolonial archaeologies look at the impact on both the colonizers and colonized in areas such as power and ethnogenesis. The field has clear implications for contemporary economic imperialism. (see **Ideology, Subaltern** & Chap. 5)

Postmodernism. A philosophy and method of analysis that (among other things) rejects the traditional structure of scientific investigation and scientific authority itself. "Incredulity towards metanarratives" is how François Lyotard defined it, which is about as succinct a definition as I can think of. He meant that human behavior is historically contingent—the result of conditions at a particular time and place—rather than the result of the operation of general principles (such as ecology) or 'laws' of human behavior. (see **Metanarrative, Modernism** & Chap. 1)

Postprocessual. Any number of interpretive archaeologies that emerged from a rejection of the scientific, generalizing goals of processual archaeology. Some postprocessual approaches were heavily influenced by **postmodern** theory (see **New Archeology** & Chap. 1)

Poststructuralism. An intellectual movement that rejected the linguistics-based model of structuralism. From a situation where things' meanings could at least in theory be deduced by systematic structural analysis, poststructuralism's effect on archaeology has to been to emphasize the **contextual, multivocal,** and **writerly** meaning of artifacts. (see Chap. 1 & 10)

Practice theory. It may seem odd to have a theory of practice, but there it is. The idea is based on Marx's idea of praxis—putting ideas to work in society. Practice theory seeks to discover how societies reproduce themselves and change. Material culture plays a significant role in this process by means of its recursive quality, and the ways in which individual actors use objects to implement their own strategies. With its emphasis on **agency** and historical **context,** practice theory contrasts with the processual concern with structure and large-scale processes. (see **Postprocessual, Poststructuralism, Structuration** & Chap. 9)

Problematize. To examine a generally held assumption as questionable. For example, **queer theory** has problematized the assumption of **heteronormalcy** in history and culture. (see Chap. 7)

Processualism. An archaeological approach that seeks to explain the role of cultural processes in human history. (see **Postprocessualism** & Chap. 1)

Proletariat. The social class that does not own the means of production, lives by wage work, and has no stake in the capitalist economy. (see **Marxism** & Chap. 3)

Queer theory. A contrarian approach that emphasizes everything that is at variance with normative culture. It is often concerned with marginalized sexual and gender groups, although any group or practice considered deviant could just as easily be the subject of study. More that anything else, queering archaeology involves taking seriously peoples, practices, and thoughts that are unthinkable in normative culture. (see **Transgressive** & Chap. 7)

Readerly/Writerly. **Roland Barthes** used *readerly* to mean writing and art that uses familiar conventions (such as a linear storyline or a tree that looks like a tree) that fulfill readers' expectations of what a book or art should be like. Reading this kind of book provides **pleasure** because it is passive act. *Writerly* work on the other hand is disruptive. It challenges the reader to see reality without the intervening structure and creates the sensation Barthes calls **jouissance** (bliss). This idea of disrupting conventional views, of disregarding established categories, is the essence of **postmodernism**. (see Chap. 10)

Recursive. Artifacts are said to be 'recursive' because they don't just sit there and reflect the values of the society that made them but actively influence human actions. (see Chap. 4)

Reflexive. Has nothing to do with your doctor thumping on your knee with a little rubber mallet. Rather, it means constantly operating in a self-aware, self-critical manner to continually reassess what you are doing and why you are doing it. According to Ian Hodder, reflexivity begins "at the trowel's edge," long before interpretation. That is, it starts with the field archaeologist's on-the-spot definition of what does and does not constitute data.

Relational analogy. An analogy that is supported by a cultural or historical connection between two elements of a culture (such as artifacts or subsistence practices). That two groups use a similar looking artifact doesn't mean they use it for the same purpose. A relational analogy provides a stronger case by grounding the analogy in ethnography or history. (see **Direct Historical Approach** & Chap. 1 & 8)

Resistance. Active defiance of a dominant ideology through acts of personal agency. Acts of resistance may include **transgressive** clothing, work slowdowns, and outright revolution. (see **Hegemony, Structuration** & Chap. 5 & 9)

Role. The set of behaviors members of a culture expect of an individual in a particular context. Among the roles that one might take on in a given day are: child (in relation to a parent regardless of your age), worker bee (in relation to your boss), boss (in relation to that new employee), and passenger (in relation to others on the bus). **Gender** roles are those expected of us because of either our gender or, more insidiously, our biological sex.

Sartre, Jean-Paul (jhon-*pol* sart-*ruh*). The most celebrated French philosopher of the twentieth century. Sartre was an existentialist. That means he rejected **essentialism**, the idea that people have an inherent characteristic or 'essence' that determines human potential. I mention him here for his **Marxist** interpretation of history. Sartre's book, *Anti-Semite and Jew,* even makes the case that anti-Semitism is the product of capitalism. (see Chap. 3)

Scientific method. The process by which a testable hypothesis is derived from a theory and tested using field data. The results of the test are used to refine the hypothesis, which is tested again.

Structuralism. This theory posits that the human mind (and consequently society and culture) is structured in the same rule-governed way as language. This is a sort of law-and-order way of looking at human psychology and culture that proposes an innate human proclivity to see reality in terms of a series of oppositional relationships: up/down, raw/cooked, male/female. (see **Poststructuralism** & Chap. 8)

Structuration. A made-up word, courtesy of English sociologist Anthony Giddens, who uses it to describe the relationship between individuals and the social structures in which they live. Giddens suggests that although these structures limit their options, people are not mere passive blobs. They have **agency** and actively go after what they want. This collision of agency and structure is the cause of social change, says Lord Giddens. He is said by some political lefties to have been made a baron (a British lord) in recognition of his service to neoliberalism. You may think that. I couldn't possibly say. (see Chap. 9)

Subaltern. A member of the politically un-selfaware mass of people, the subaltern class. One goal of postcolonial archaeology is to identify **agency** among subaltern peoples. (see **Antonio Gramsci** & Chap. 5)

Teleology. A model that presupposes an outcome or ultimate result. **Functionalist** interpretations tend to be teleological—since the functionalist feels that he or she knows why a particular trait is present, the evidence is construed as supporting the initial premise. Strict **historical materialist** interpretations that see history as the inevitable march towards a post-capitalist world are teleological. (see Chap. 2)

Text. **Postmodernist**-influenced archaeology owes a lot to **Roland Barthes**'s concept of the text. Although it originally referred to written sources, the term soon came to refer to a range of non-linguistic things from fashion to photographs, and to artifacts both archaeological and contemporary. What they have in common is their ability to be read (interpreted) as if they were texts. Texts, like archaeological artifacts, can be **deconstructed** to reveal new meanings. And following his **Death of the Author** idea, Barthes disallows even the creator of a text (or the user of an artifact) the final word on what it means. It's a fixed principle of postmodern-influenced archaeology that there's no final, definitive 'reading' of the meaning of an artifact. Which leaves the archaeologist with the decision to read the artifact/text in either a **readerly** or a **writerly** way. (see Chap. 10)

Thick description. An ethnographic method devised by **Clifford Geertz** that uses in-group knowledge and close observation to interpret individual acts at the small scale. (see Chap. 11 & 14)

TLDR. Acronym for "too long, didn't read." Applied to an internet post that is excessively wordy or that the reader just doesn't have the time or interest to plow through.

Tradition, archaeological. A set of artifact types that indicate the use of a particular technology or behavioral complex over a long period of time, such as the Australian Small Tool tradition.

Transgressive. Ways of thinking, acting, or understanding that transgress cultural norms. A transgressive reading of an erotic magazine may extract meanings about the commodification of women; thus, a **text** that is apparently **univocal** turns out to be nothing of the sort given the right analysis. What constitutes a transgressive act is in constant flux. The tattoos, colored hair, and piercings of English punks were outrageously transgressive when they appeared in the 1980s. However, the shock value of these accoutrements dissolved as they found their way into the suburban mall and were, thus, co-opted as **normative** fashion accessories. Today, they hardly provoke a raised eyebrow, pierced or otherwise. (see **Deconstruction, Queer theory, Text, Multivocality** & Chap. 10)

Writerly. (see **Readerly**)

With the right partner, the Venus of Willendorf
was surprisingly light on her feet.

INDEXES

Index of Ideas

Index of People

ABOUT THE AUTHOR/ILLUSTRATOR

Adrian Praetzellis's professional career started in 1972 when he began digging full-time on Roman and medieval sites on the British archaeological circuit. This led to work on prehistoric and eighteenth/nineteenth-century archaeology in Virginia, the Great Basin, and California, where he has lived ever since.

Adrian has a Ph.D. in Anthropology from UC Berkeley and is Professor of Anthropology at Sonoma State University. In addition to teaching archaeology and cultural resources management, he is Director of the Anthropological Studies Center, a university research institute. Adrian is author/illustrator of *Death by Theory* and *Dug to Death* (AltaMira Press, 2000 [2011] and 2003). The latter has been celebrated as "the only archaeology textbook with a Yiddish glossary"—a claim to fame that's unlikely to be challenged any time soon.